ROCK SONGS
FOR KIDS

ISBN 978-1-4950-2835-9

HAL•LEONARD®
CORPORATION

7777 W. BLUEMOUND RD. P.O. BOX 13819 MILWAUKEE, WI 53213

ALL SHOOK UP

Words and Music by OTIS BLACKWELL
and ELVIS PRESLEY

With a Shuffle beat

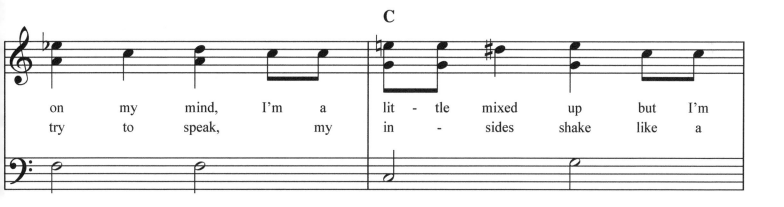

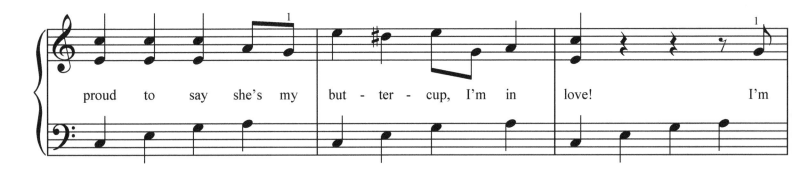

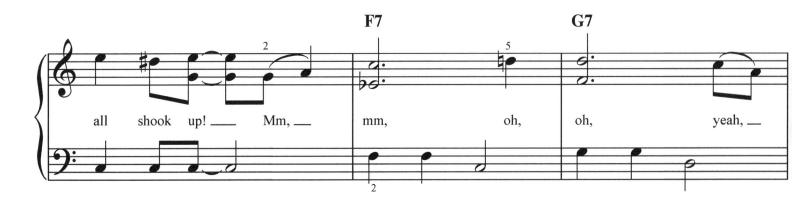

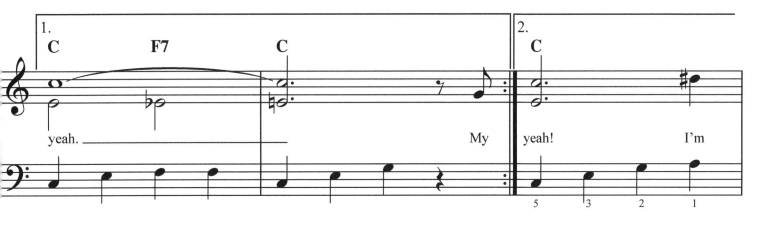

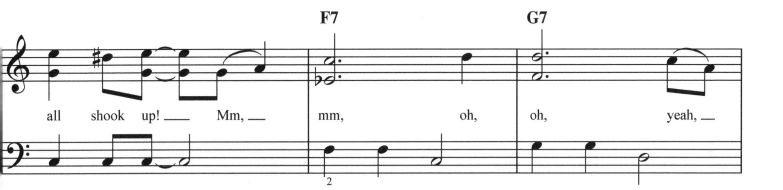

BEAT IT

Words and Music by
MICHAEL JACKSON

Moderately fast

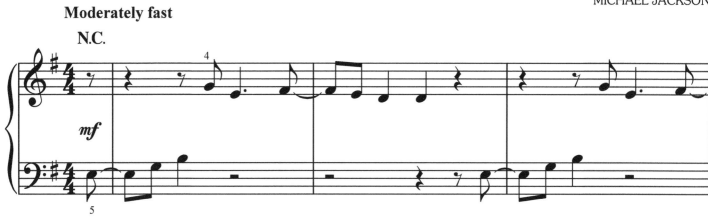

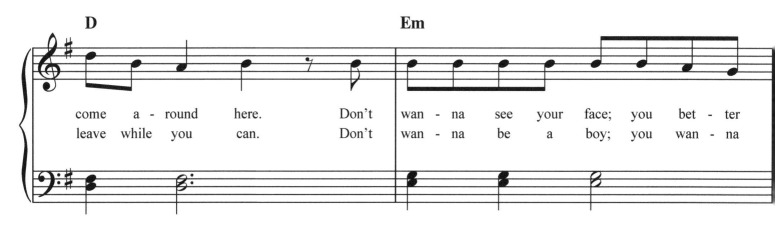

They told him, "Don't you ev - er
They're out to get you. Bet - ter
Instrumental

come a - round here. Don't wan - na see your face; you bet - ter
leave while you can. Don't wan - na be a boy; you wan - na

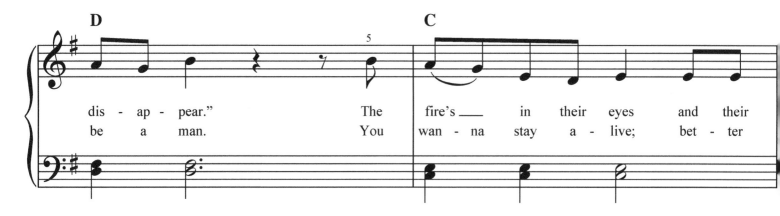

dis - ap - pear." The fire's ___ in their eyes and their
be a man. You wan - na stay a - live; bet - ter

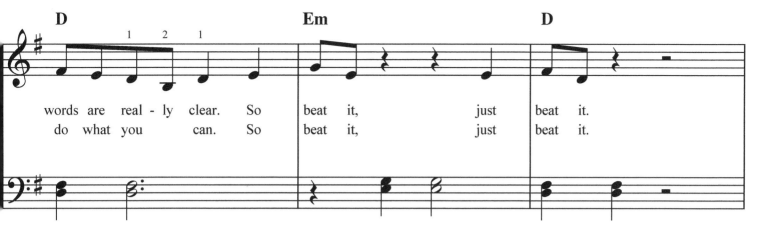

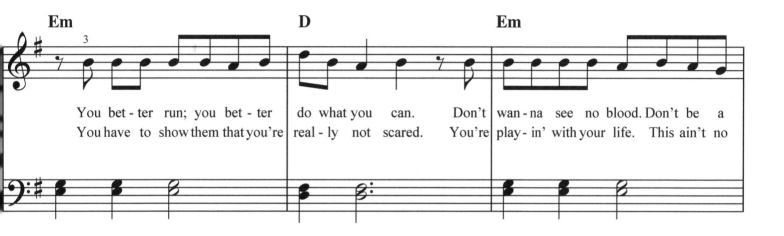

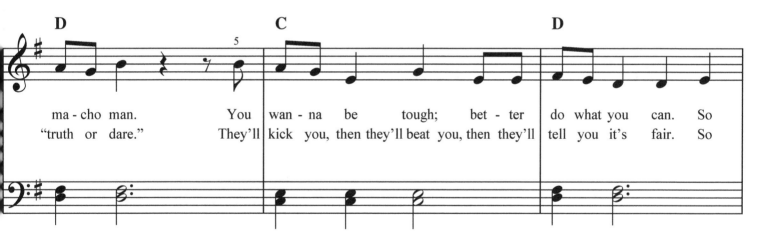

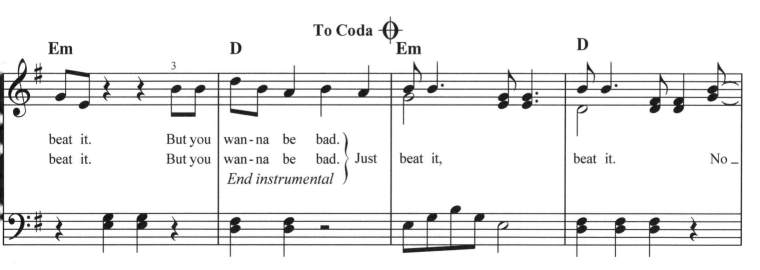

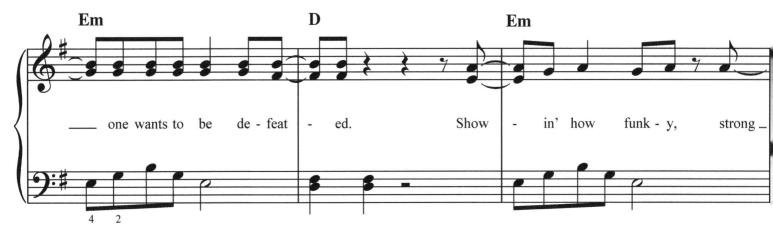

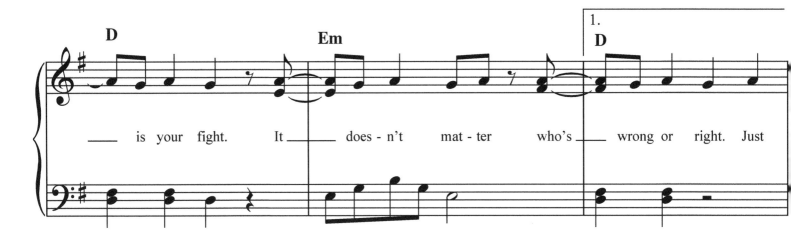

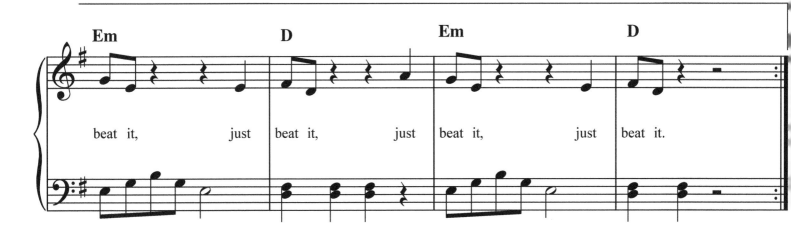

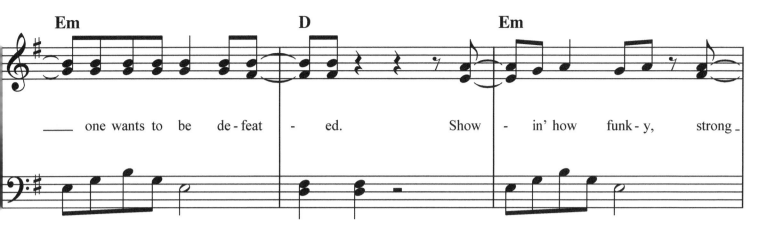

_____ one wants to be de - feat - ed. Show - in' how funk - y, strong _____

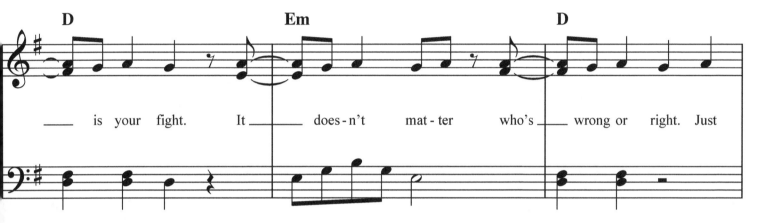

_____ is your fight. It _____ does - n't mat - ter who's _____ wrong or right. Just

beat it. Beat it.

Beat it. Beat it.

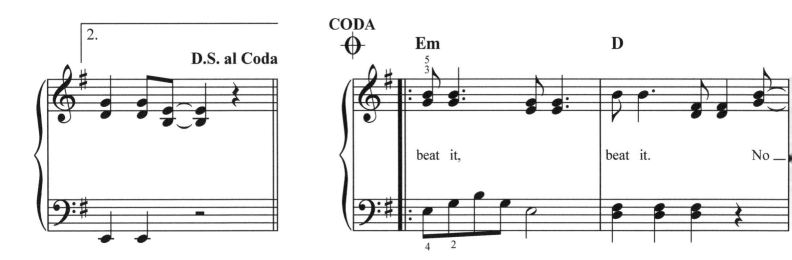

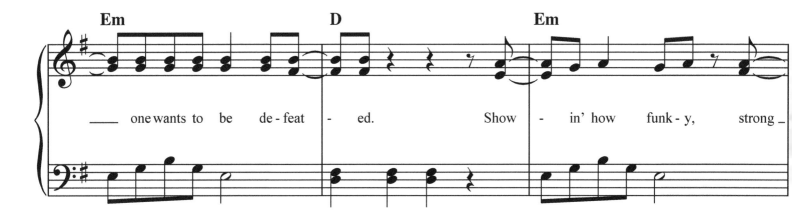

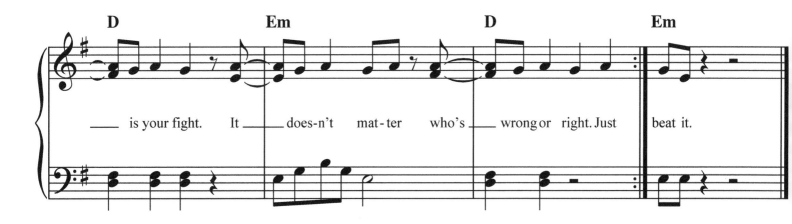

BEAUTIFUL DAY

Words by BONO
Music by U2

Moderately

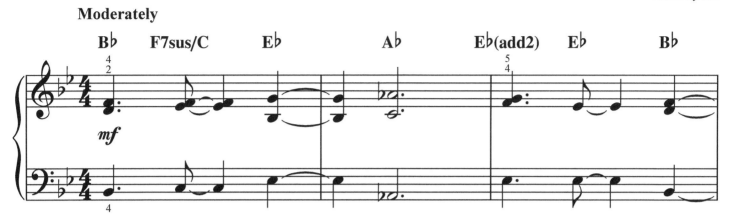

The heart is a bloom, ___ shoots

up through the ston-y ground. ___ But there's no room, ___

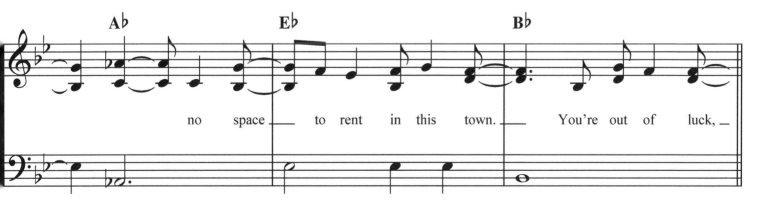

no space ___ to rent in this town. ___ You're out of luck, ___

12

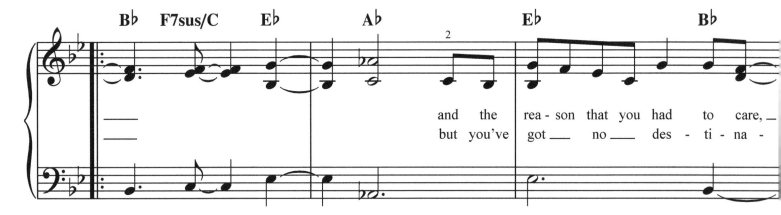

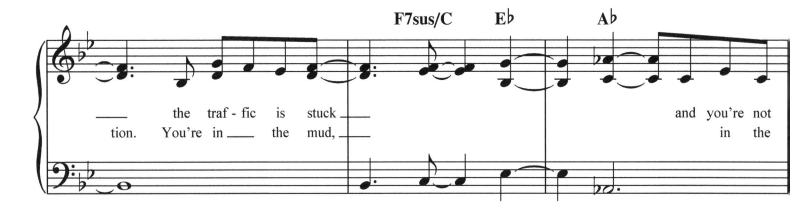

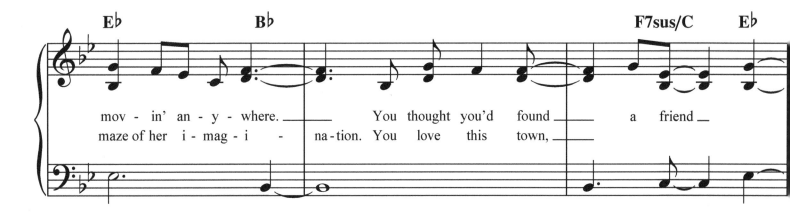

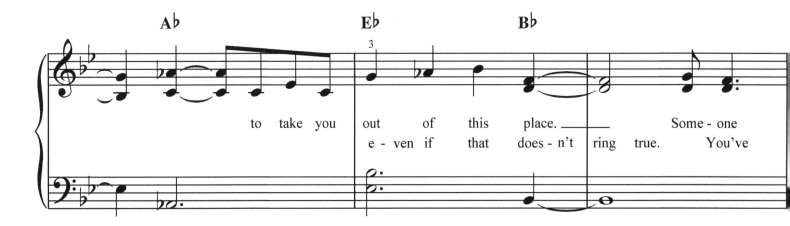

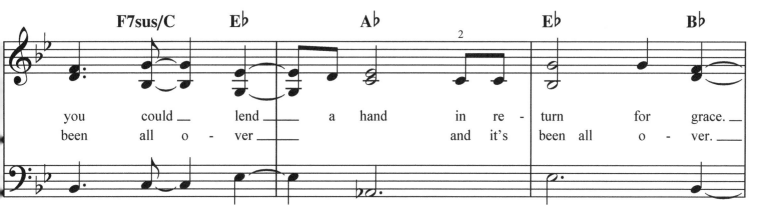

you could ___ lend ___ a hand in re - turn for grace. ___
been all o - ver ___ and it's been all o - ver. ___

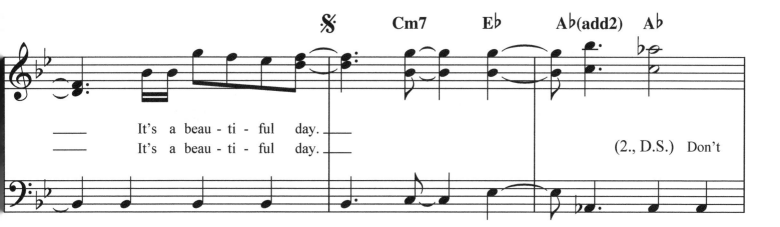

___ It's a beau - ti - ful day. ___
___ It's a beau - ti - ful day. ___

(2., D.S.) Don't

The sky falls, you feel ___ like it's a beau - ti - ful day. ___
let it get a - way. ___ A beau - ti - ful day. ___

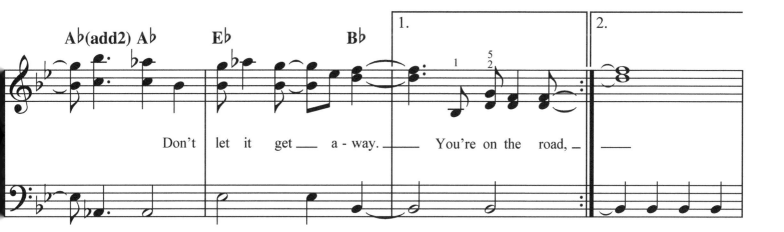

Don't let it get ___ a - way. ___ You're on the road, ___

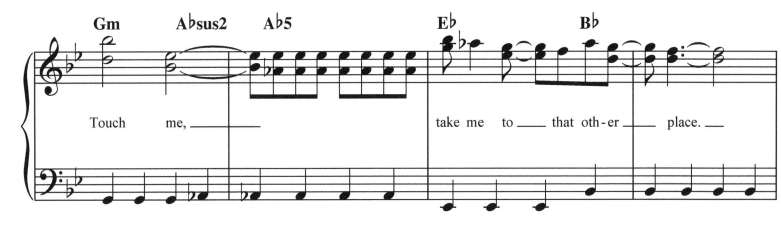

Touch me, _____ take me to ___ that oth-er ___ place. __

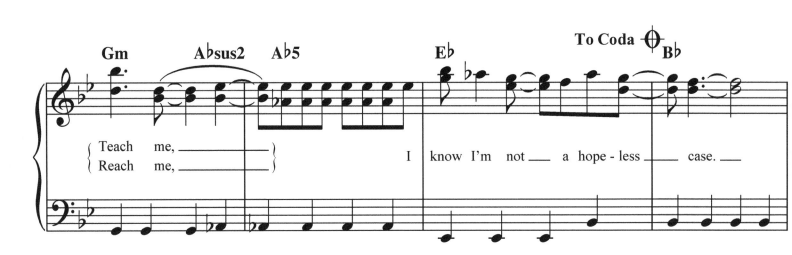

Teach me, _____
Reach me, _____ I know I'm not ___ a hope-less ___ case. __

To Coda ⊕

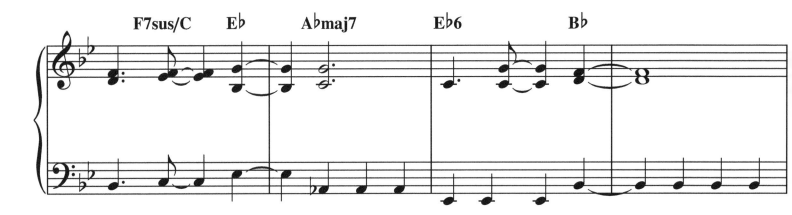

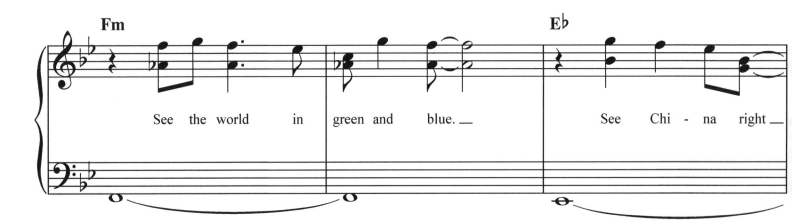

See the world in green and blue. __ See Chi - na right __

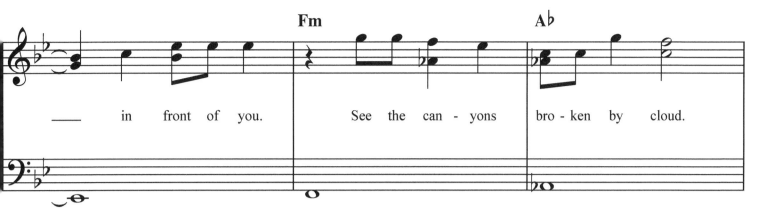

in front of you. See the can - yons bro - ken by cloud.

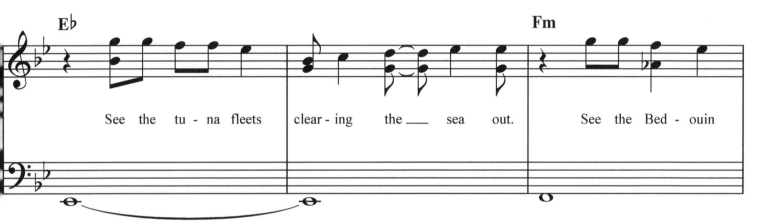

See the tu - na fleets clear - ing the ___ sea out. See the Bed - ouin

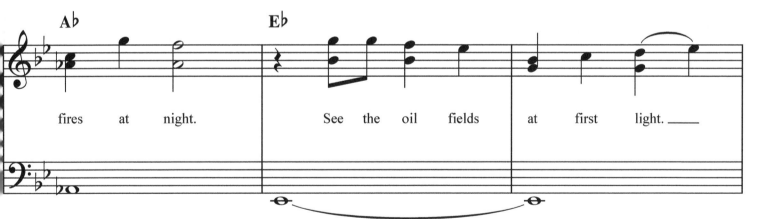

fires at night. See the oil fields at first light. ___

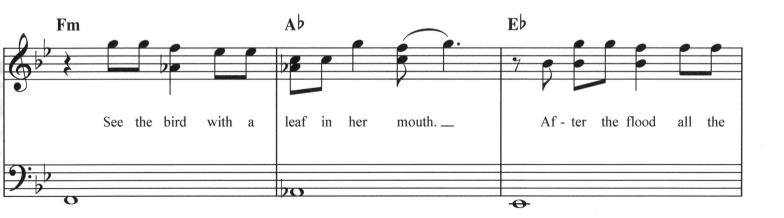

See the bird with a leaf in her mouth. ___ Af - ter the flood all the

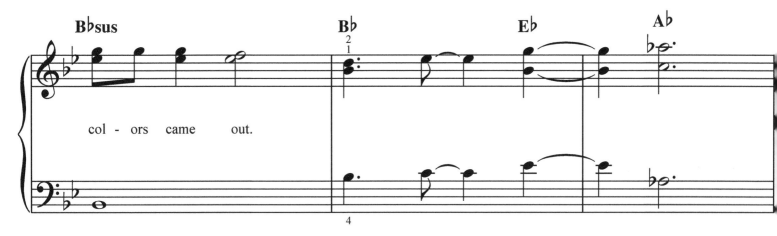

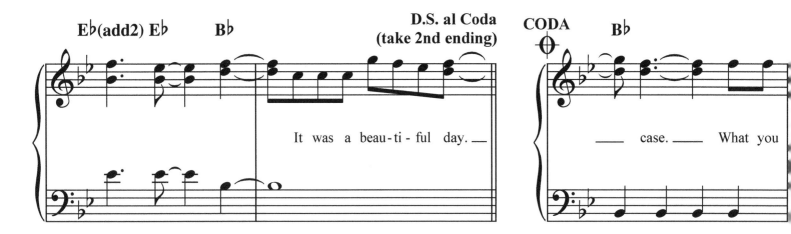

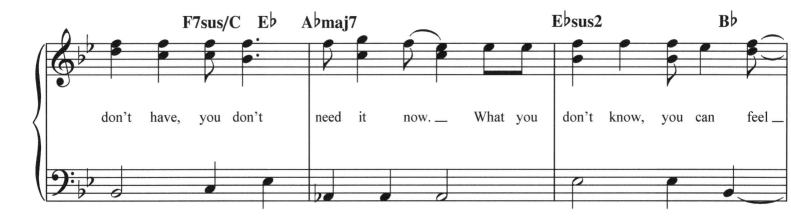

need it now. _____ It's a beau - ti - ful day.

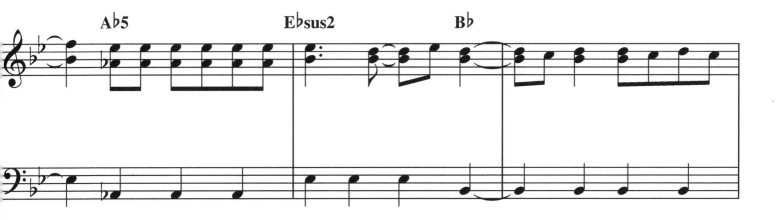

rit.

CRAZY LITTLE THING CALLED LOVE

Words and Music by
FREDDIE MERCURY

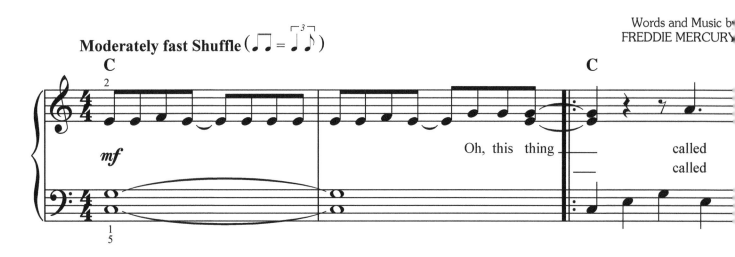

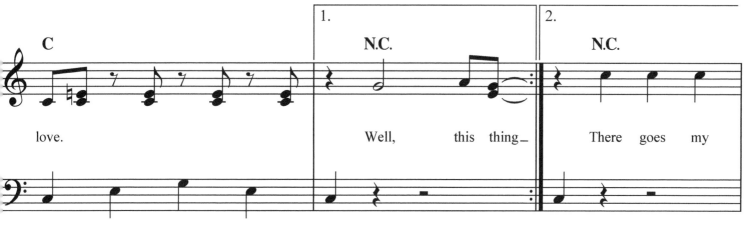

love.　　Well,　this thing —　There goes my

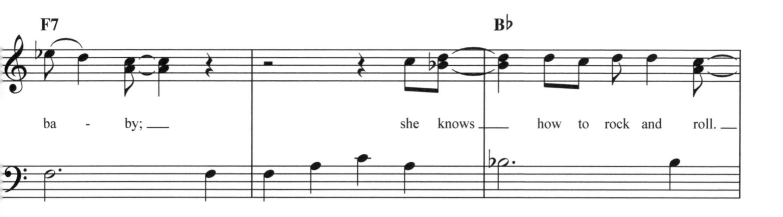

ba - by; —　she knows —　how to rock and roll. —

— She drives — me cra - zy. —　She gives me

hot and cold fe - ver. She leaves me in a cool, cool sweat.

I got - ta be cool, __

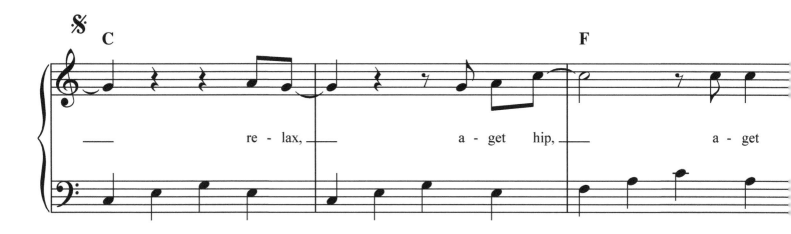

__ re - lax, __ a - get hip, __ a - get

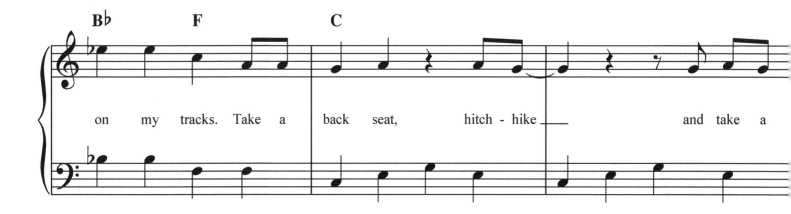

on my tracks. Take a back seat, hitch - hike __ and take a

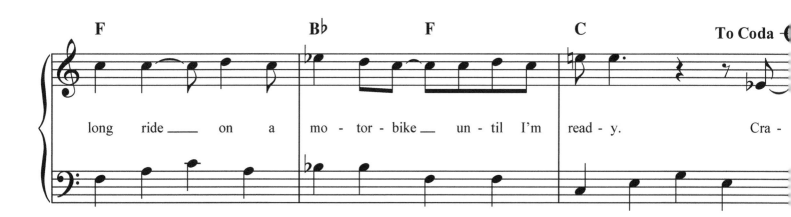

long ride __ on a mo - tor - bike __ un - til I'm read - y. Cra -

- zy lit - tle thing called love.

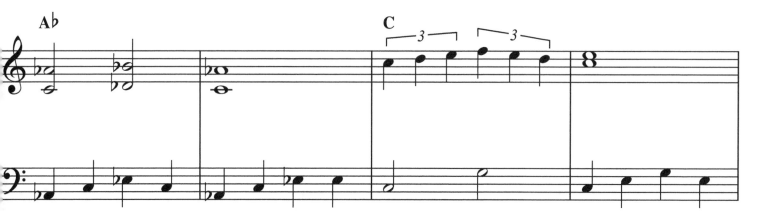

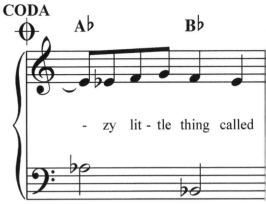

D.S. al Coda

I got - ta be cool,__

CODA

A♭ **B♭**

- zy lit - tle thing called

C

love.

This thing____ called

F **B♭** **F**

love, I____ just_____ can't__ han - dle it.__ This

C **F**

thing called love, I____ must____ get a-

round to it.____ I ain't__ read - y. Cra - zy lit - tle thing called

love, cra - zy lit - tle thing called love, cra -

- zy lit - tle thing called love, cra - zy lit - tle thing called

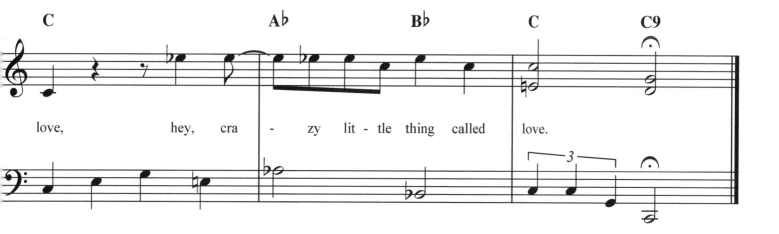

love, hey, cra - zy lit - tle thing called love.

I GOT YOU
(I Feel Good)

Words and Music by
JAMES BROWN

Moderate Funk

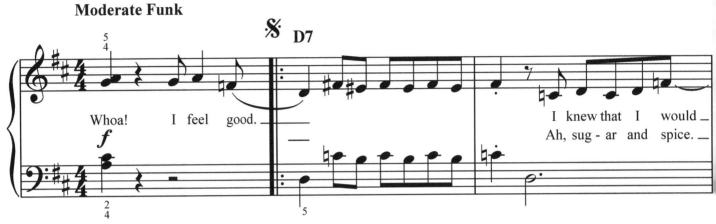

Whoa! I feel good. ___
I knew that I would ___
Ah, sug - ar and spice. ___

___ now.
I feel ___ good.
I feel ___ nice.

I knew that I would ___ now.
Ah, sug - ar and spice. ___
So good,
So nice,

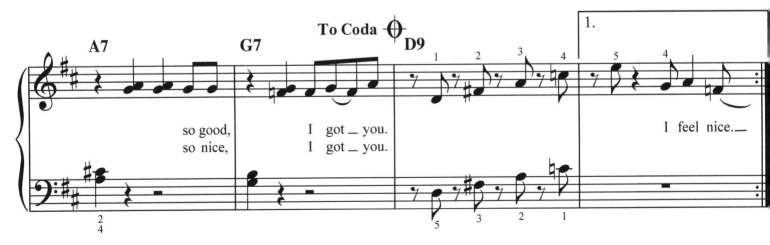

so good,
so nice,
I got ___ you.
I got ___ you.
I feel nice. ___

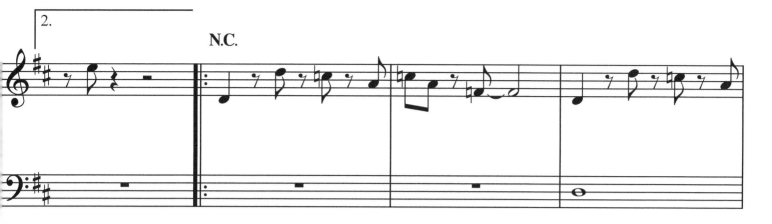

When I hold _ you in my arms, I know that I can do no

wrong. _____ And when I hold _ you in my arms, my

{ love won't do you no harm. _____ }
{ love can't do me no harm. _____ }

And I feel _____ nice. _____

Ah, sug - ar and spice.   I feel _____

G7   **D7**

nice.   Ah, sug - ar and spice. _____

A7   **G7**

So nice,   so nice,   I got ____ you.

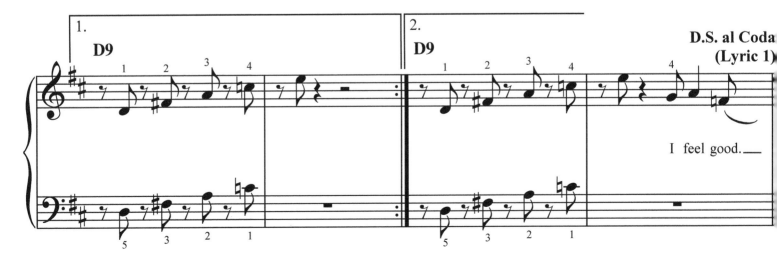

1.
D9

2.
D9

D.S. al Coda
(Lyric 1)

I feel good. ____

CODA

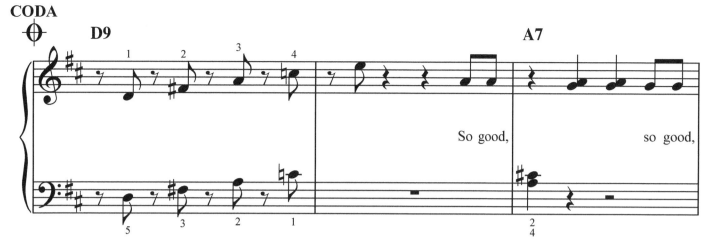

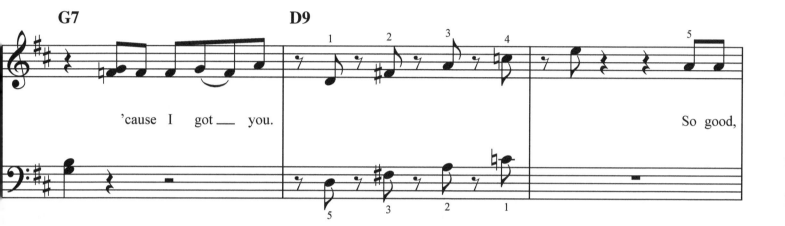

I LOVE ROCK 'N ROLL

Words and Music by ALAN MERRILL
and JAKE HOOKER

Moderately

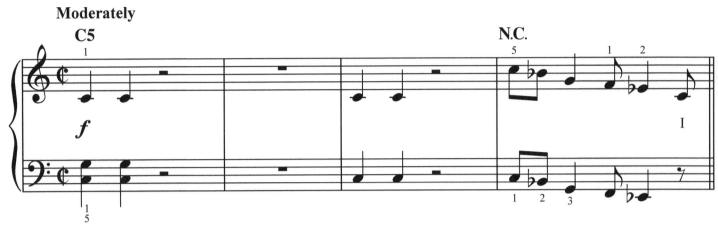

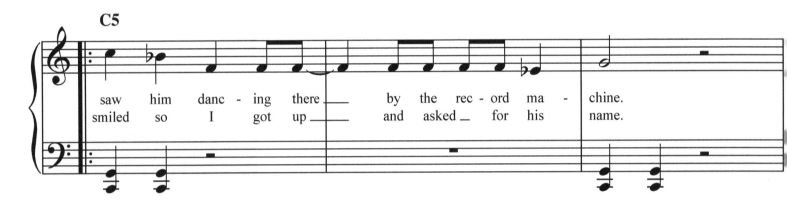

saw him danc - ing there ____ by the rec - ord ma - chine.
smiled so I got up ____ and asked ___ for his name.

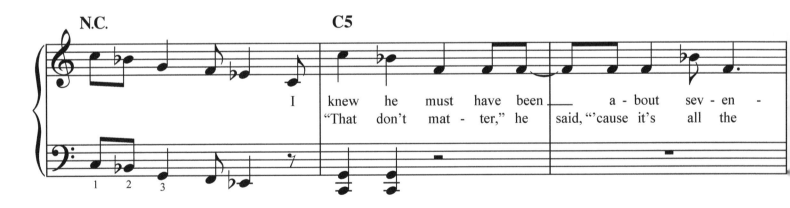

I knew he must have been ____ a - bout sev - en -
"That don't mat - ter," he said, "'cause it's all the

teen.
same."

The beat was go - ing strong, ____
I said, "Can I take you home ____

play - ing my fa-v'rite song, and I could
where we can be a - lone?" And

tell it would-n't be long ___ till he was with me, yeah,
next, we were ___ mov - ing on, and he was with me, yeah,

me. And I could tell it would-n't be long ___ till he was with
me. And next we were ___ mov - ing on, and he was with

me, yeah, me, sing - in' } I love
me, yeah, me, sing - in' }

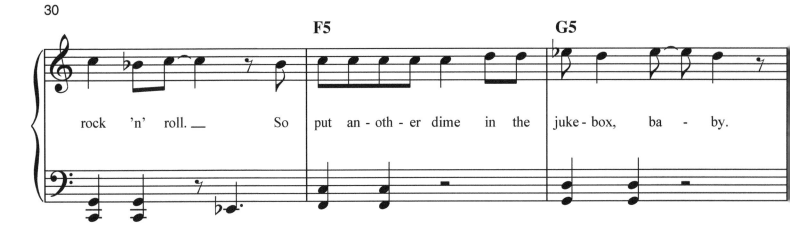

rock 'n' roll. __ So put an - oth - er dime in the juke - box, ba - by.

I love rock 'n' roll. __ So come and take your time and

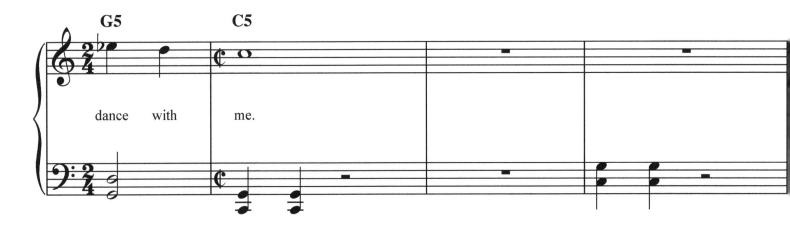

dance with me.

1.
N.C.

2.
N.C.

**D.S. al Coda
(2nd verse)**

He

I

CODA

dance with me.

LET THERE BE ROCK

Words and Music by RONALD SCOTT,
ANGUS YOUNG and MALCOLM YOUNG

No one knew ___ what they was gon - na do, ___ but Tchai - kov - sky had the news.

He said, let there be light, ___
and there was light. ___
and there was drums. ___

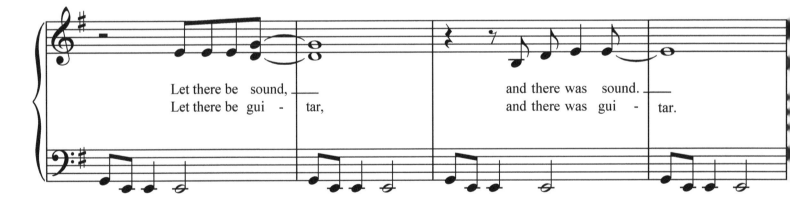

Let there be sound, ___
Let there be gui - tar,
and there was sound. ___
and there was gui - tar.

1.

Let there be drums, ___

2.

A7

Let there be rock! ___

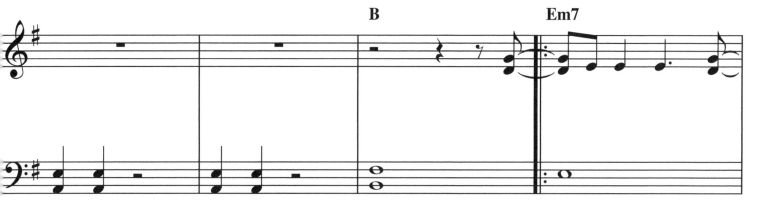

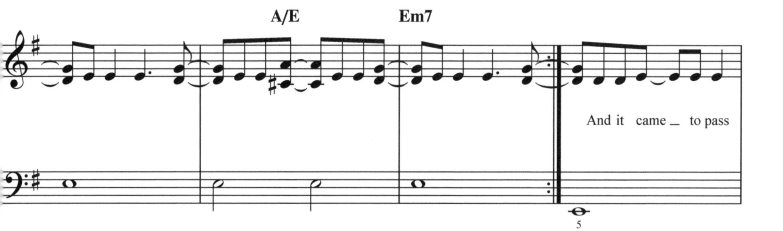

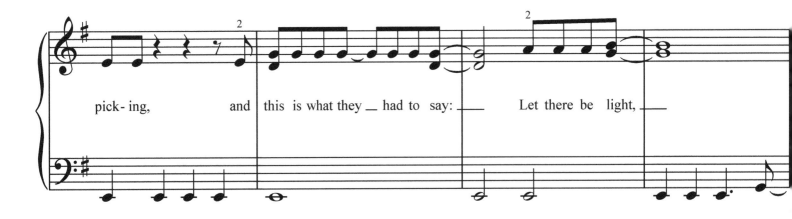

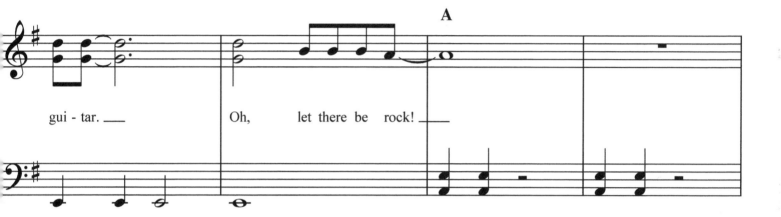

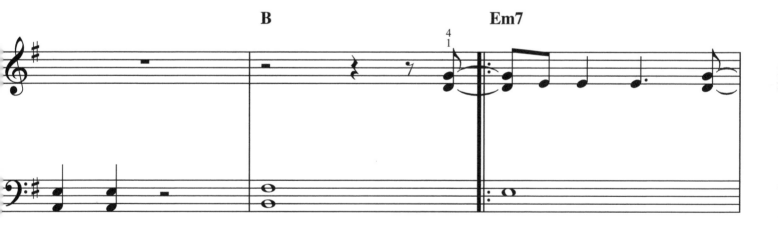

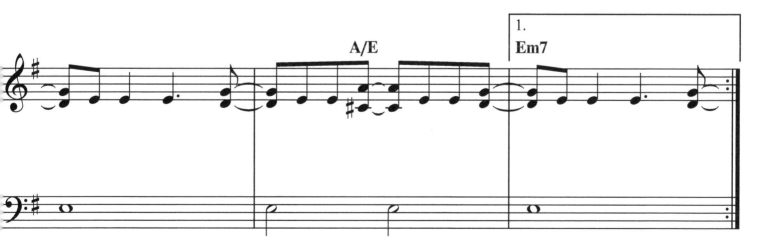

One night in a club called the Shak-ing Hand

there was a for-ty-two dec-i-bel

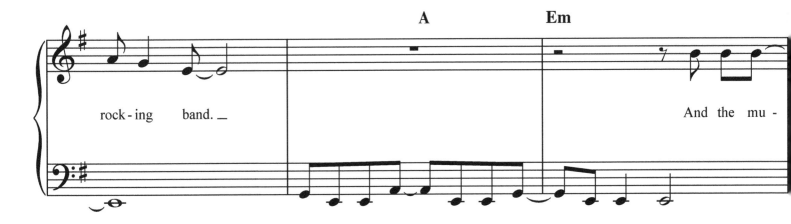

rock-ing band. And the mu-

- sic was good and the mu - sic was loud.

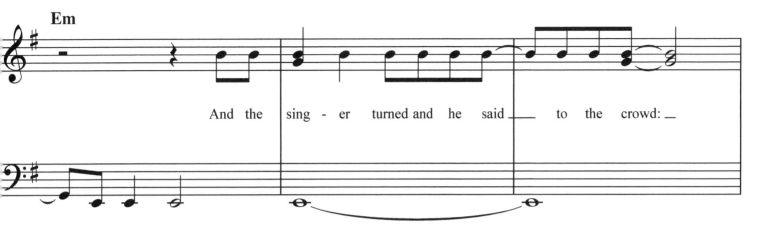

And the sing - er turned and he said ___ to the crowd: __

Let there be rock! __

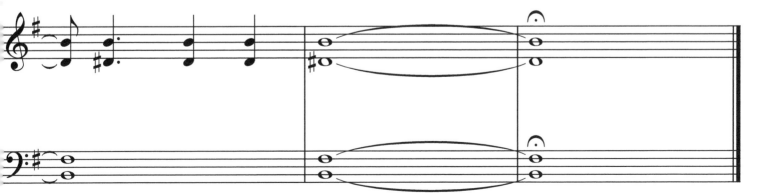

I'M A BELIEVER

Words and Music by
NEIL DIAMOND

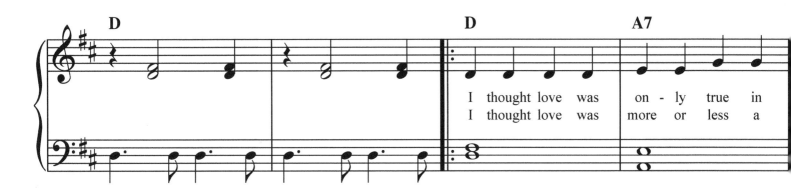

I thought love was   on - ly true in
I thought love was   more or less a

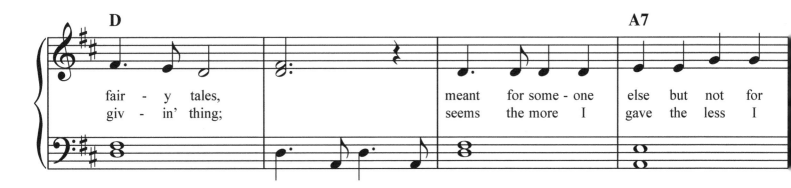

fair - y tales,   meant   for some - one   else but not for
giv - in' thing;   seems   the more I   gave the less I

me.   Love   was out to   get me.
got.   (2., D.S.) What's   the use in   try - in'?

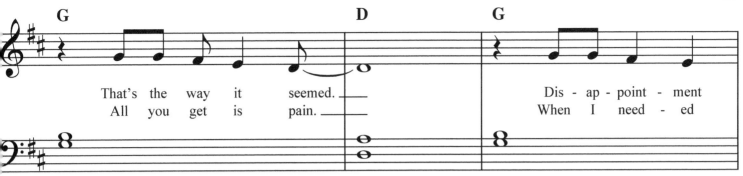

That's the way it seemed. _____
All you get is pain. _____
Dis - ap - point - ment
When I need - ed

haunt - ed all my dreams.
sun - shine I got rain.
Then I saw her face; _____

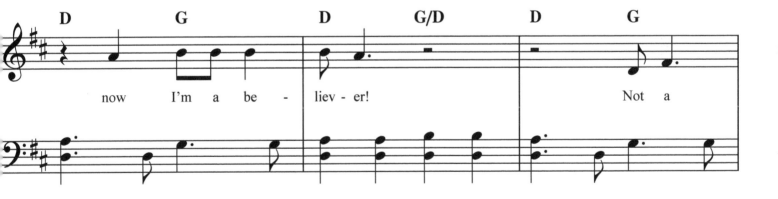

now I'm a be - liev - er!
Not a

trace _____ of doubt _ in my mind. _____ I'm in

love,   and I'm a be - liev - er! I could - n't

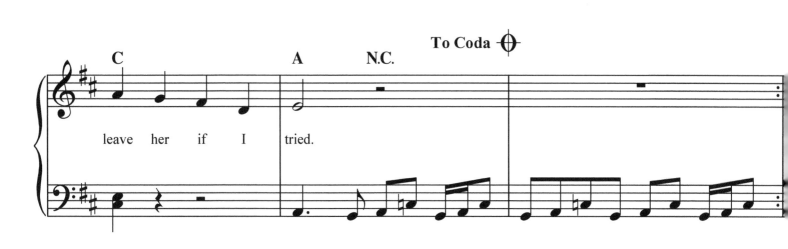

To Coda ⊕

leave her if I   tried.

_ff_

D.S. al Coda

CODA

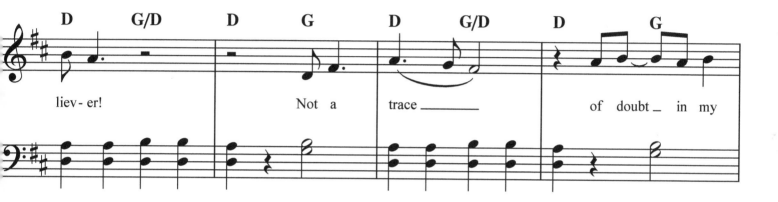

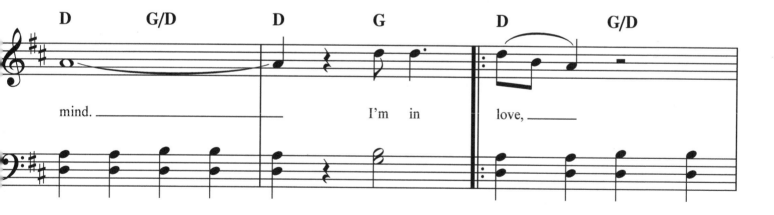

Repeat and Fade | **Optional Ending**

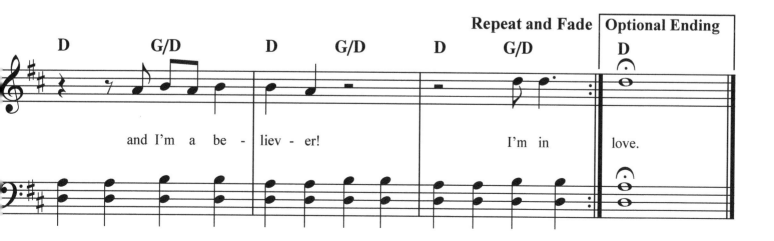

IT MUST BE LOVE

Words and Music by
LABI SIFFRE

I nev - er thought ___
How can it be ___
Instrumental

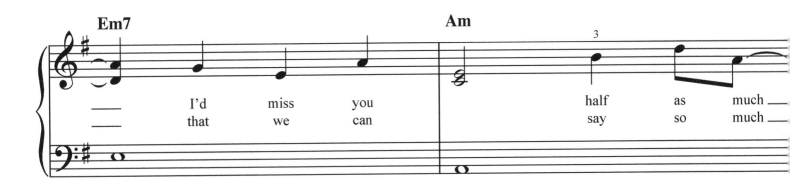

___ I'd miss you ___ half as much ___
that we can say so much ___

as I do. ___
with - out words?

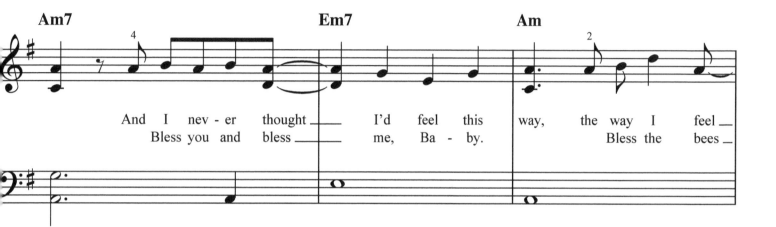

And I nev - er thought ____ I'd feel this way, the way I feel ____
Bless you and bless ____ me, Ba - by. Bless the bees ____

____ a - bout you.
____ and the birds.

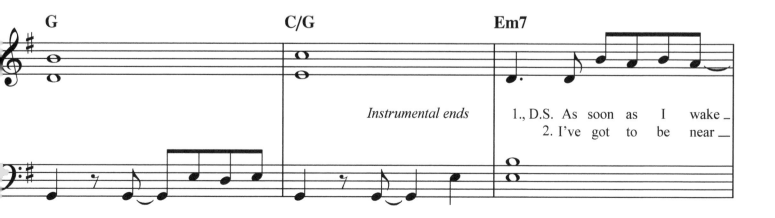

Instrumental ends 1., D.S. As soon as I wake ____
2. I've got to be near ____

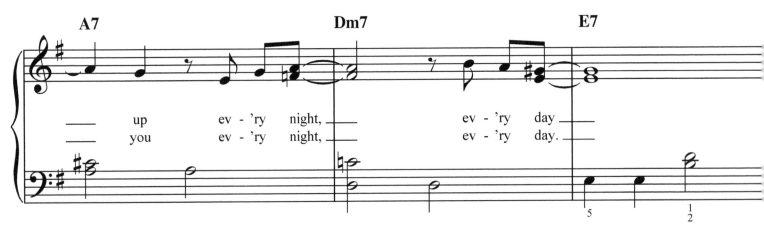

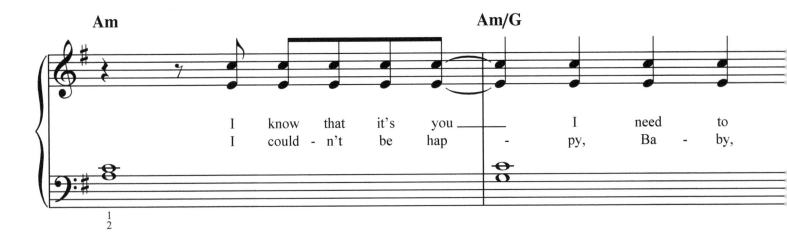

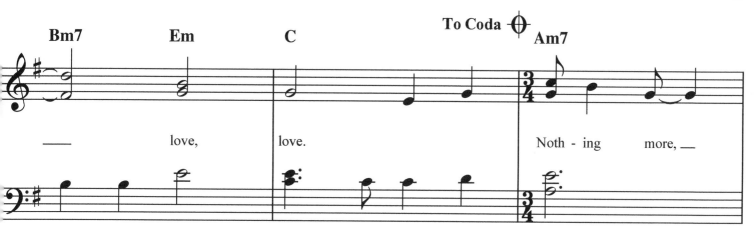

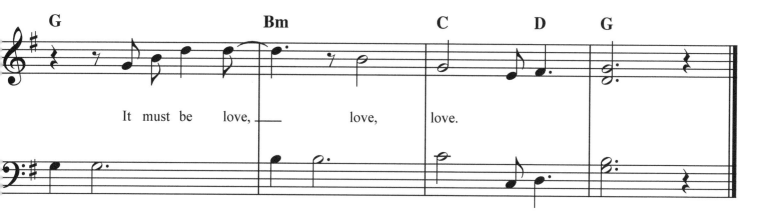

MONSTER MASH

Words and Music by BOBBY PICKETT
and LEONARD CAPIZZI

Medium Rock beat

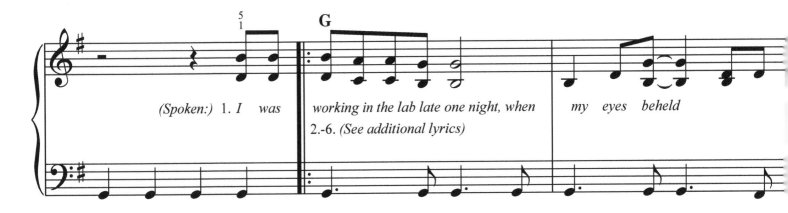

(Spoken:) 1. I was working in the lab late one night, when my eyes beheld
2.-6. (See additional lyrics)

an eerie sight, for my monster from his slab began to rise, and

suddenly,   to my surprise,   *(Sung:)* { he / they } did the

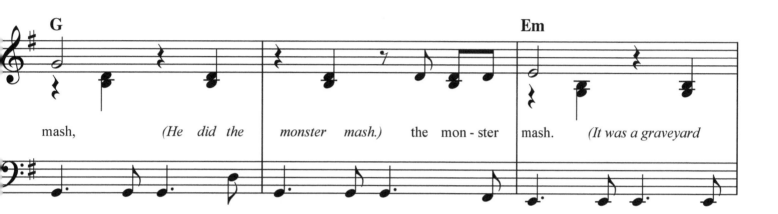

mash,   *(He did the*   *monster mash.)* the mon-ster mash.   *(It was a graveyard*

smash.)   { He / They } did the   mash, *(It caught on in*   *a flash.)*   he did the

mash.   *(He did the*   *monster mash.)* *(Spoken:)* 2. From my   *monster mash.)*

Repeat and Fade | **Optional Ending**

Additional Lyrics

2. From my laboratory in the castle east
   To the master bedroom where the vampires feast,
   The ghouls all came from their humble abodes
   To catch a jolt from my electrodes.
   Chorus

3. The zombies were having fun,
   The party had just begun.
   The guests included Wolf-man,
   Dracula, and his son.
   Chorus

4. The scene was rockin'; all were digging the sounds,
   Igor on chains, backed by his baying hounds.
   The coffin-bangers were about to arrive
   With their vocal group, "The Crypt-Kicker Five."
   Chorus

5. Out from his coffin, Drac's voice did ring;
   Seems he was troubled by just one thing.
   He opened the lid and shook his fist,
   And said, "Whatever happened to my Transylvanian Twist?"
   Chorus

6. Now everything's cool, Drac's part of the band.
   And my monster mash is the hit of the land.
   For you, the living, this mash was meant too,
   When you get to my door, tell them Boris sent you.
   Chorus

LOOKIN' OUT MY BACK DOOR

Words and Music by
JOHN FOGERTY

mag - i - na - tion sets in, pret - ty soon __ I'm
di - no - saur __ Vic - tro - la lis - t'ning to __ Buck
Both - er me __ to - mor - row, to - day I'll buy __ no

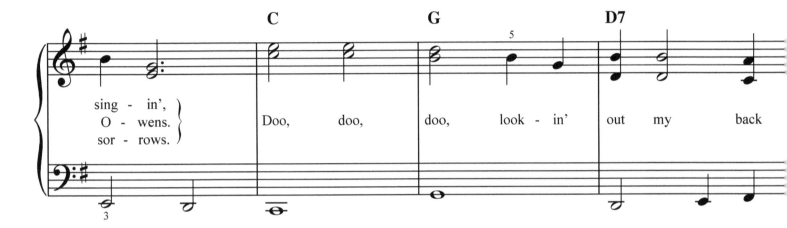

sing - in',
O - wens.   Doo, doo, doo, look - in' out my back
sor - rows.

1.
G
door.   There's a

2.
G   To next strain
door.

3.
G   Fine
door.

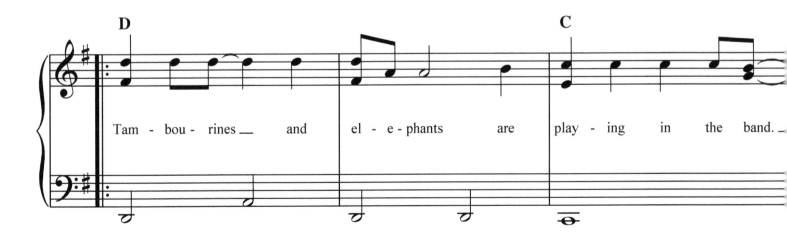

D
Tam - bou - rines __ and el - e - phants are play - ing in the band. __

Won't you take a ride ___ on the fly - in' spoon?

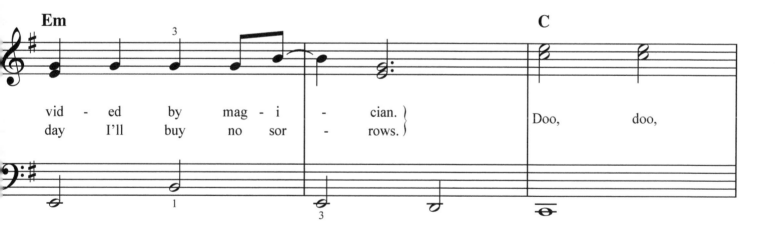

Won - d'rous ap - pa - ri - tion pro -
Both - er me to - mor - row, to -

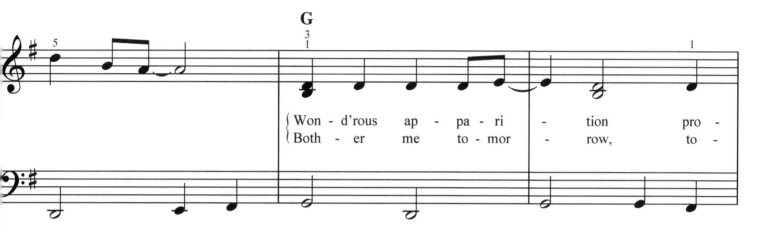

vid - ed by mag - i - cian.
day I'll buy no sor - rows.

Doo, doo,

doo, look - in' out ___ my back door.
door.

NEW KID IN TOWN

Words and Music by JOHN DAVID SOUTHER,
DON HENLEY and GLENN FREY

Moderately

There's talk on the street; __
You look in her eyes; __

__ it sounds so fa - mi - liar.
__ the mu - sic be - gins to play.

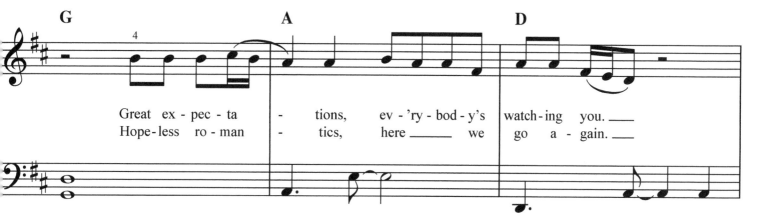

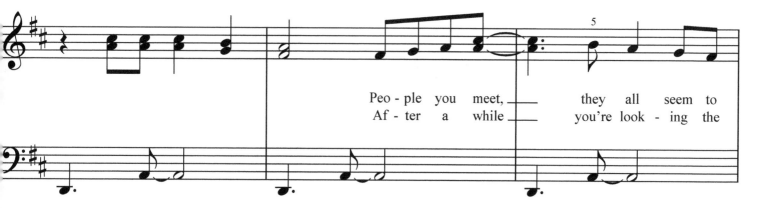

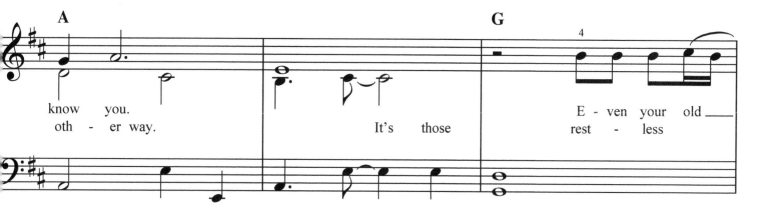

Johnny-come-late - ly, the new kid in
Johnny-come-late - ly, the new kid in

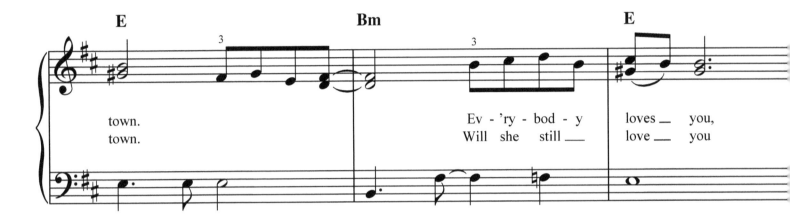

town.
town. Ev - 'ry - bod - y loves ___ you,
Will she still ___ love ___ you

so don't let them down. ___ when you're not a -

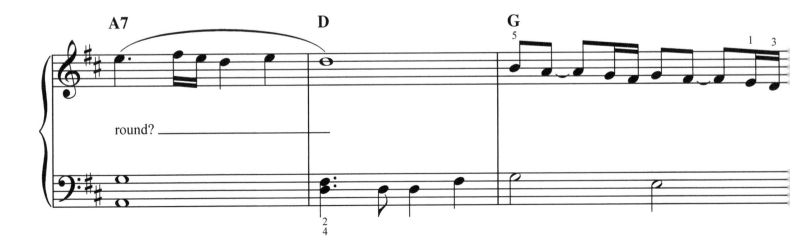

round? ___

There's so man - y things you should have told _____ her,

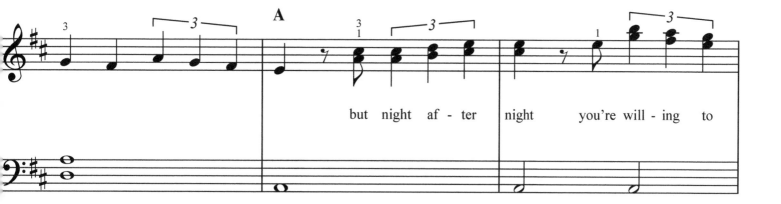

but night af - ter night you're will - ing to

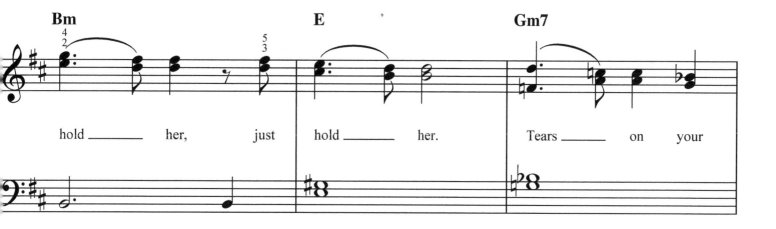

hold _____ her, just hold _____ her. Tears _____ on your

shoul - der. There's talk on the street; it's there to re-

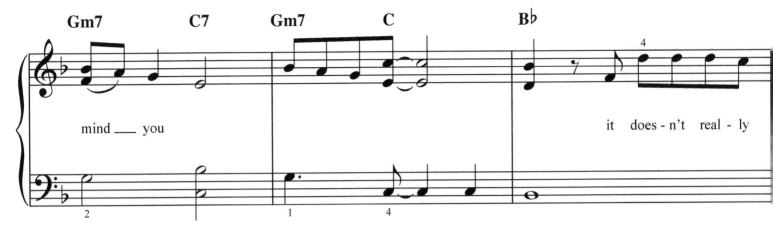

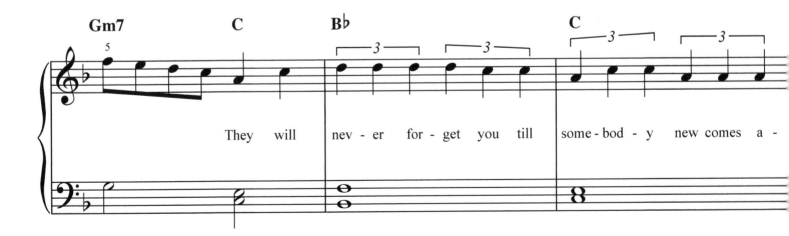

long. _____

Where you been

late - ly?

There's a new kid in town.

Ev - 'ry - bod - y loves _ him, don't _ they? _____

Now he's hold - ing

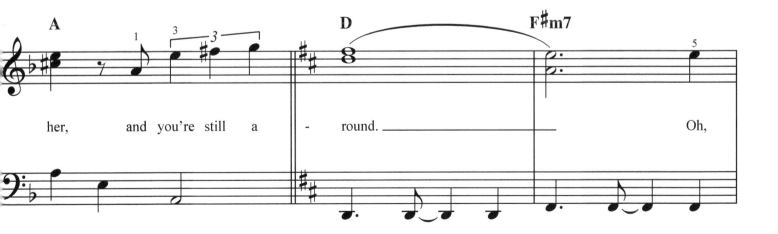

her, and you're still a - round. _____

Oh,

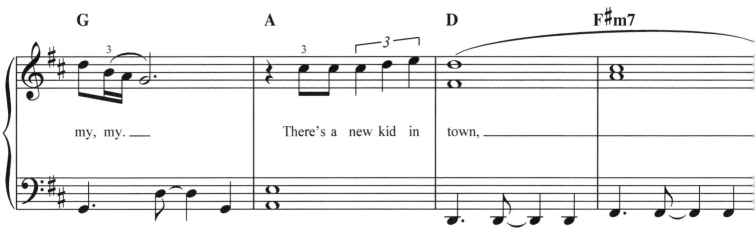

my, my. ____   There's a new kid in   town, ____

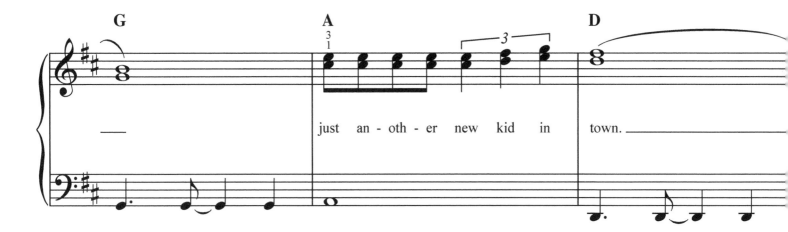

____   just an-oth-er new kid in   town. ____

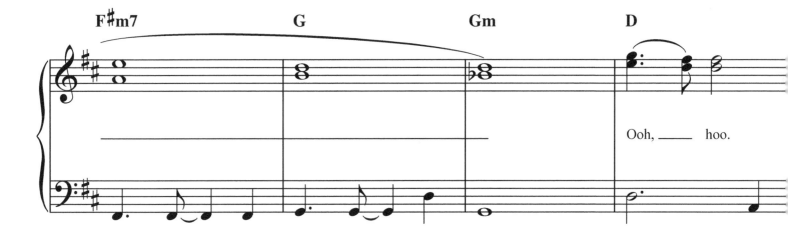

Ooh, ____ hoo.

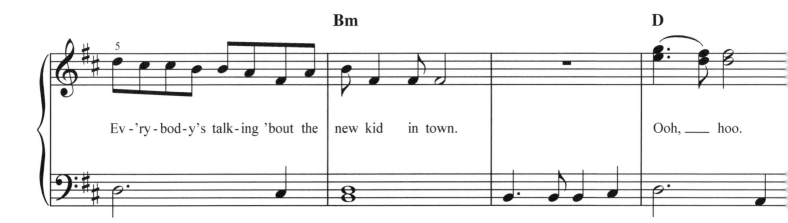

Ev-'ry-bod-y's talk-ing 'bout the   new kid   in town.   Ooh, ____ hoo.

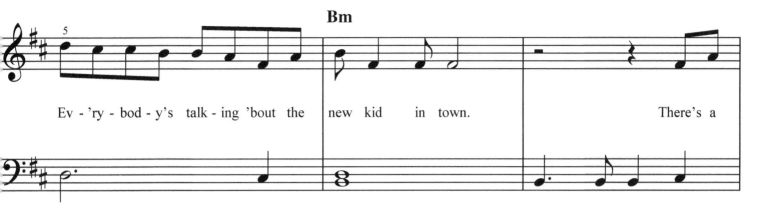

Ev - 'ry - bod - y's talk - ing 'bout the new kid in town. There's a

new kid in town. I don't want to hear it. There's a new kid in town. I ____

____ don't want to hear it. There's a new kid in town. There's a

new kid in town. Ooh, ____ hoo. ____

ROCK AROUND THE CLOCK

Words and Music by MAX C. FREEDMAN
and JIMMY DeKNIGHT

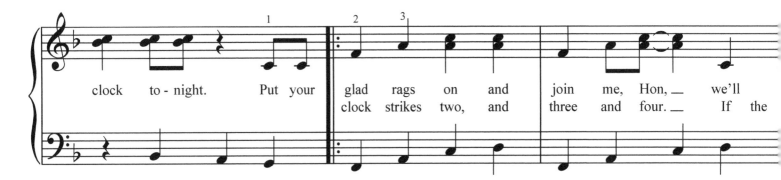

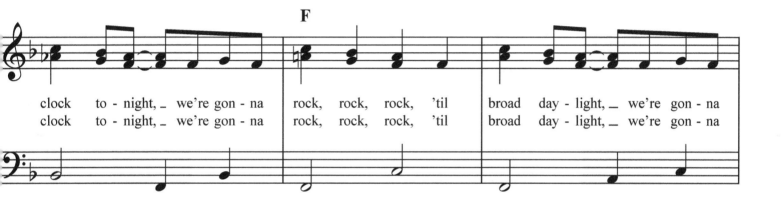

have some fun when the clock strikes one, __ we're gon - na rock a - round the
band slows down we'll __ yell for more, __ we're gon - na rock a - round the

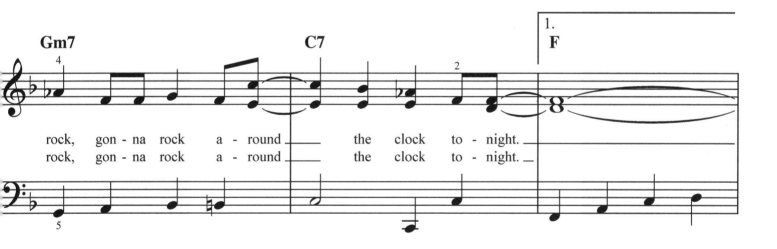

clock to - night, __ we're gon - na rock, rock, rock, 'til broad day - light, __ we're gon - na
clock to - night, __ we're gon - na rock, rock, rock, 'til broad day - light, __ we're gon - na

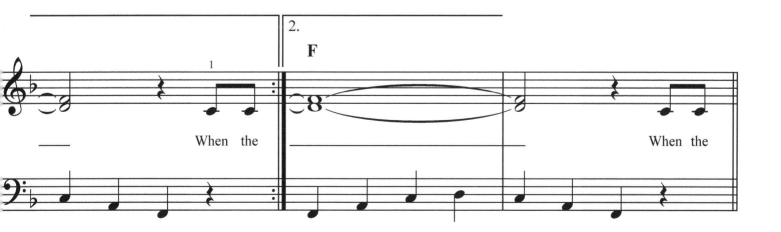

rock, gon - na rock a - round __ the clock to - night. __
rock, gon - na rock a - round __ the clock to - night. __

When the

When the

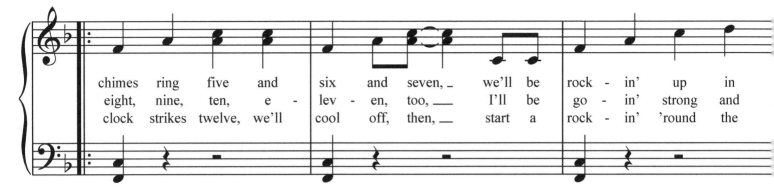

chimes ring five and six and seven, _ we'll be rock - in' up in
eight, nine, ten, e - lev - en, too, _ I'll be go - in' strong and
clock strikes twelve, we'll cool off, then, _ start a rock - in' 'round the

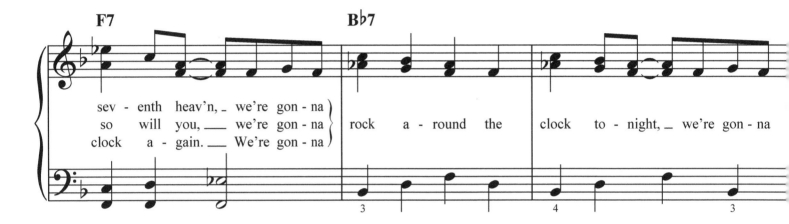

F7   Bb7

sev - enth heav'n, _ we're gon - na
so will you, _ we're gon - na   rock a - round the   clock to - night, _ we're gon - na
clock a - gain. _ We're gon - na

F   Gm7   C

rock, rock, rock, 'til broad day - light, _ we're gon - na rock, gon - na rock a - round ___ the clock to - night. _

1., 2.
F   3.
F   Bb7   F   F9

When it's
When the

THREE LITTLE BIRDS

Words and Music by
BOB MARLEY

Moderately slow Reggae

Don't

wor - ry   a - bout a   thing,   'cause

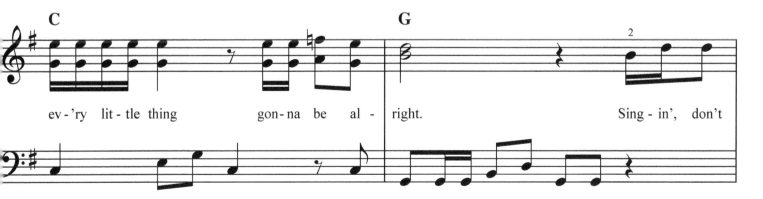

ev -'ry lit - tle thing   gon - na be al - right.   Sing - in', don't

wor - ry a - bout a thing, 'cause

ev - 'ry lit - tle thing gon - na be al - right. Rise up this

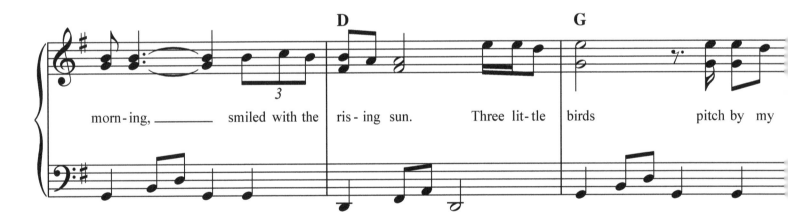

morn - ing, _____ smiled with the ris - ing sun. Three lit - tle birds pitch by my

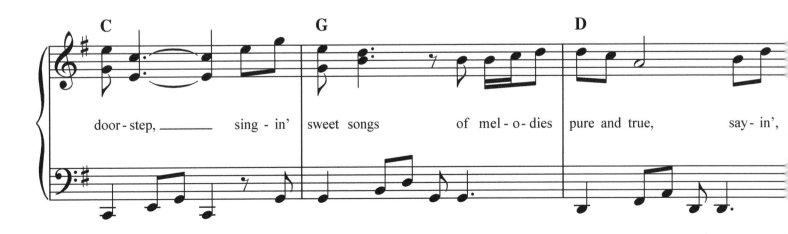

door - step, _____ sing - in' sweet songs of mel - o - dies pure and true, say - in',

"This is my mes-sage to you- oo-oo." _____ Sing-in', don't | oo-oo." _____ Sing-in', don't

wor-ry a-bout a thing, 'cause ev-'ry lit-tle thing gon-na be al-

right. Sing-in', don't wor-ry a-bout a thing, 'cause

ev-'ry lit-tle thing gon-na be al-right.

ROCK LOBSTER

Words and Music by KATE PIERSON,
FRED SCHNEIDER, KEITH STRICKLAND,
CINDY WILSON and RICKY WILSON

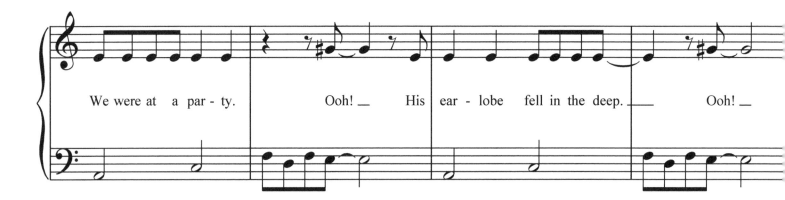

Ah,   ah,   ah,   ah.   Rock

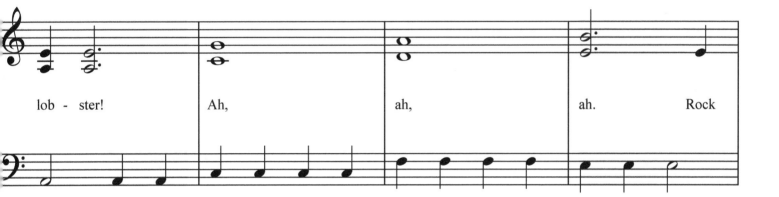

lob - ster!   Ah,   ah,   ah.   Rock

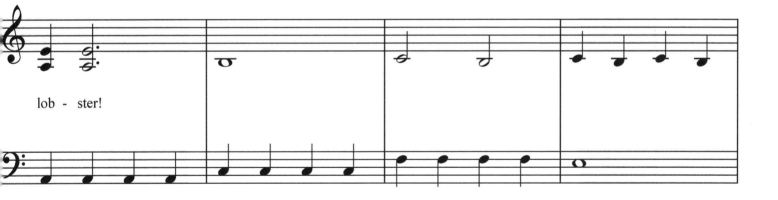

lob - ster!

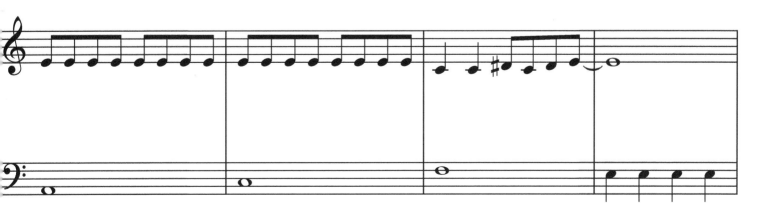

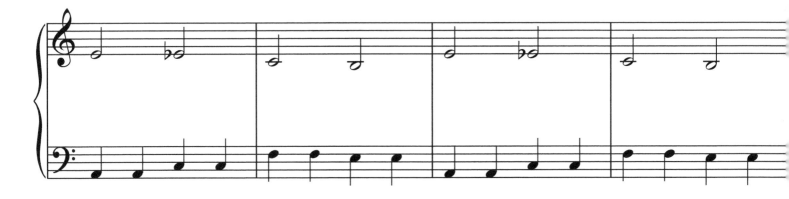

To Coda

N.C.

Ski-

doo-ba-da.   Ooh! __ Ski - doo-ba-da.   Ooh! __

We were at the beach. Ooh! — Ev-'ry-bod-y had match-ing towels. —

Some-bod-y went un-der a dock — and there they saw a rock. Ooh! —

D.S. al Coda

It was-n't a rock. Ooh! — It was a rock lob - ster! —

CODA

Rock

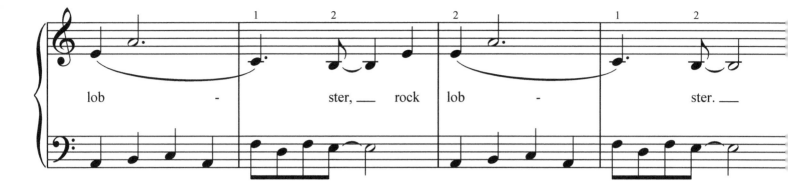

lob - ster, ___ rock lob - ster. ___

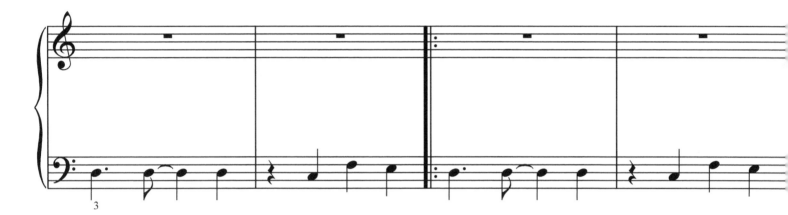

Boys in bi - ki - nis
Here comes a sting - ray,

girls in surf - boards, ___
there goes a man - ta ray.

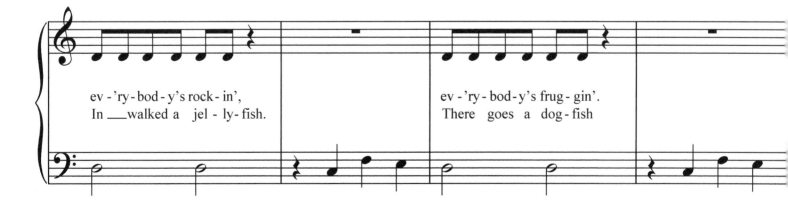

ev - 'ry - bod - y's rock - in',
In ___ walked a jel - ly - fish.

ev - 'ry - bod - y's frug - gin'.
There goes a dog - fish

Twist-ing 'round the fire, hav-ing fun, ___ In flew a sea rob-in.
chased by a cat - fish.

bak - in' po - ta - toes, bak - in' in the sun. There goes a nar - whal. _
Watch out for that pi - ran - ha!

1.

Put on your nose guard, put on your life - guard.
Here comes a bi - ki - ni.

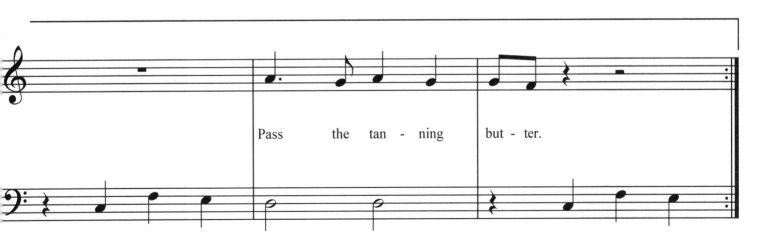

Pass the tan - ning but - ter.

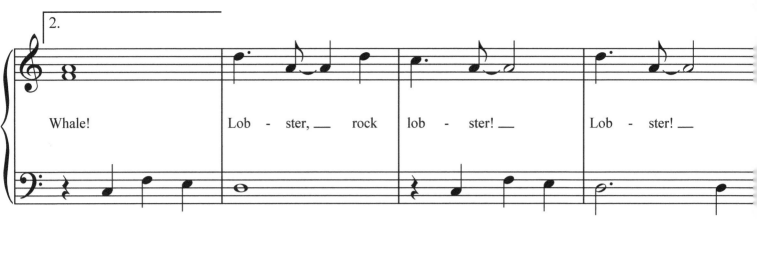

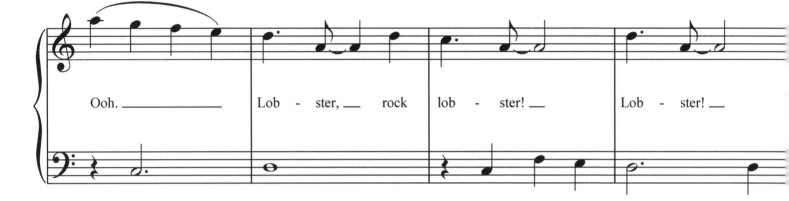

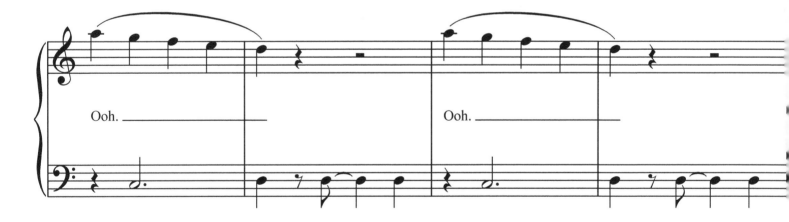

ROCK THIS TOWN

Words and Music by
BRIAN SETZER

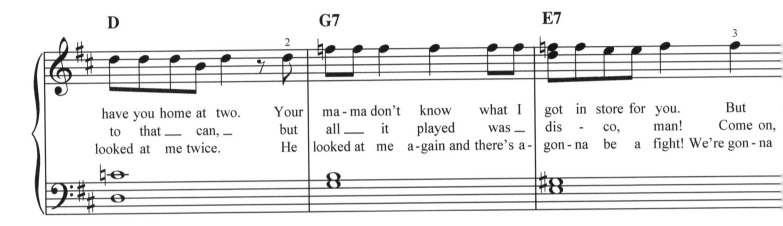

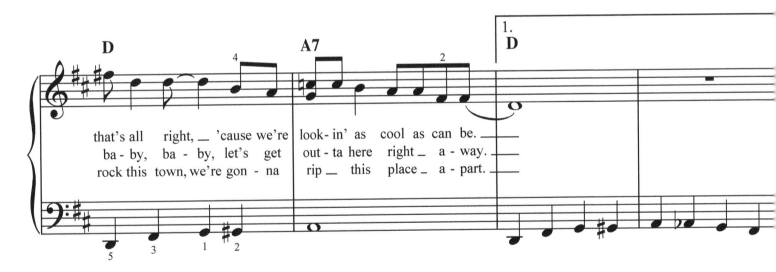

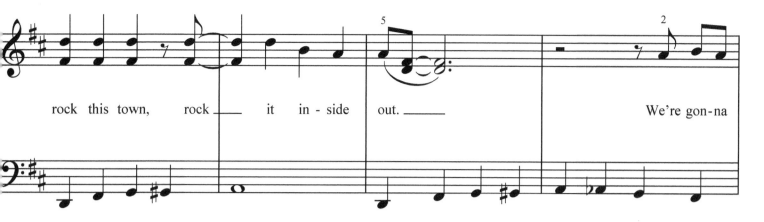

rock this town, rock ___ it in - side out. ___ We're gon-na

rock this town, make 'em scream and shout. _ Let's

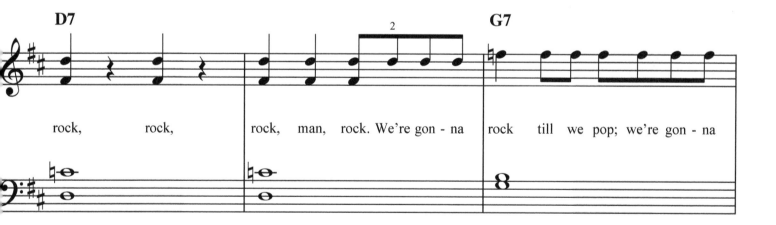

rock, rock, rock, man, rock. We're gon - na rock till we pop; we're gon - na

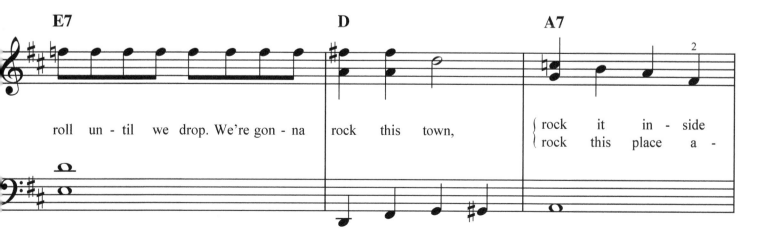

roll un - til we drop. We're gon - na rock this town, {rock it in - side / rock this place a -

To Coda ⊕   **D.S. al Coda**
(take 2nd ending)

D

out.
part.

Well, we're

CODA ⊕

We're gon - na rock this town, rock____ it in - side

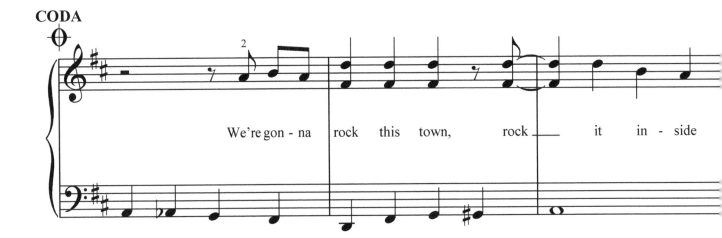

out. _____

We're gon - na rock this town,

A7   D7

make 'em scream and   shout. ___   Let's   rock,   rock,

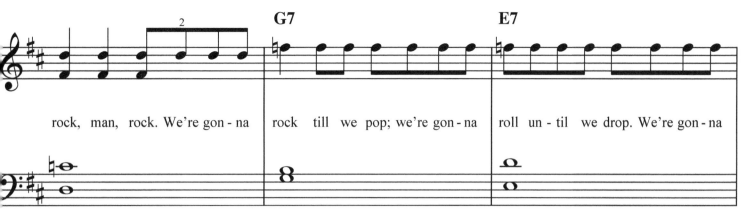

rock, man, rock. We're gon - na | rock till we pop; we're gon - na | roll un - til we drop. We're gon - na

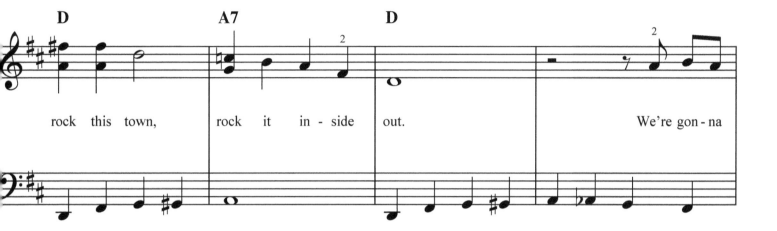

rock this town, | rock it in - side out. | | We're gon - na

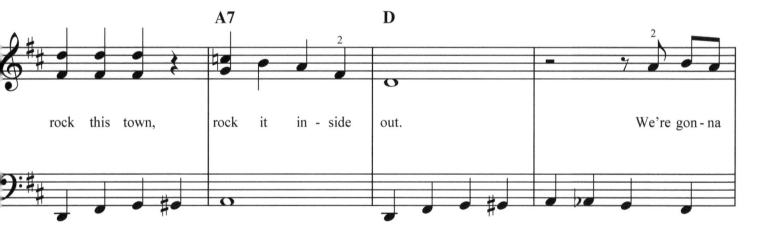

rock this town, | rock it in - side out. | | We're gon - na

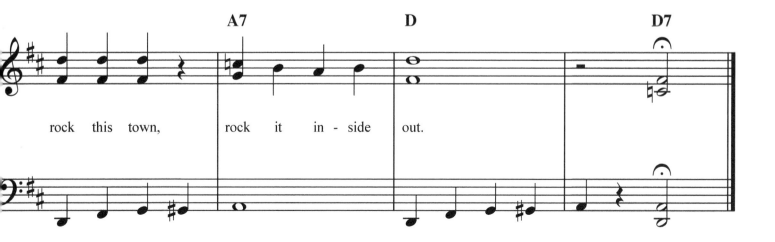

rock this town, | rock it in - side out.

SIR DUKE

Words and Music by
STEVIE WONDER

Moderately

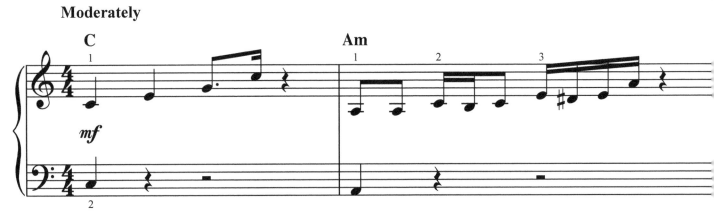

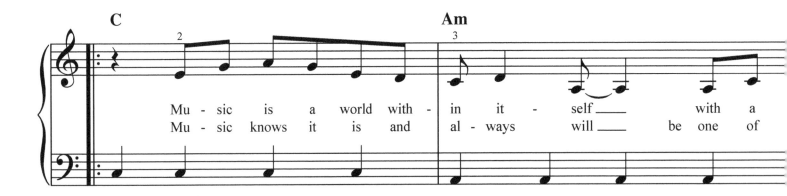

Mu - sic is a world with - in it - self ___ with a
Mu - sic knows it is and al - ways will ___ be one of

lan - guage we all un - der - stand, ___
the things that life just won't quit. ___

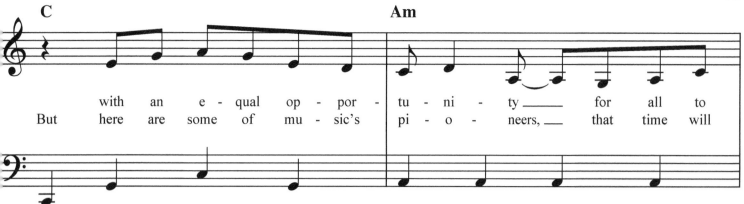

C   **Am**

with an e - qual op - por - tu - ni - ty _____ for all to
But here are some of mu - sic's pi - o - neers, ___ that time will

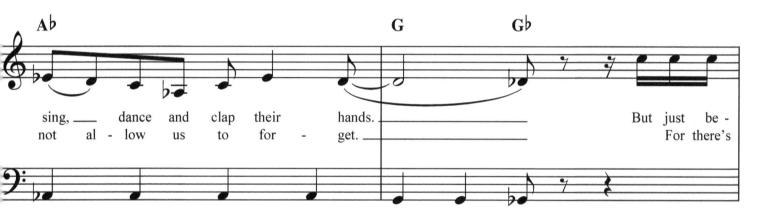

Ab   **G**   **Gb**

sing, ___ dance and clap their hands. _____ But just be -
not al - low us to for - get. _____ For there's

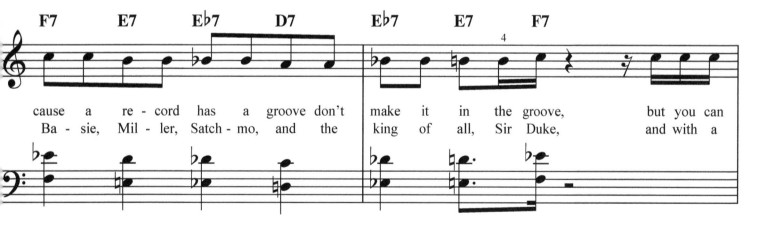

F7   **E7**   **Eb7**   **D7**   **Eb7**   **E7**   **F7**

cause a re - cord has a groove don't make it in the groove, but you can
Ba - sie, Mil - ler, Satch - mo, and the king of all, Sir Duke, and with a

       E7   **Eb7**   **D7**   **Eb** **E** **F** **F#** **G9**

tell right a - way at let - ter A when the peo - ple start to move.
voice like El - la's ring - in' out there's no way the band can lose.

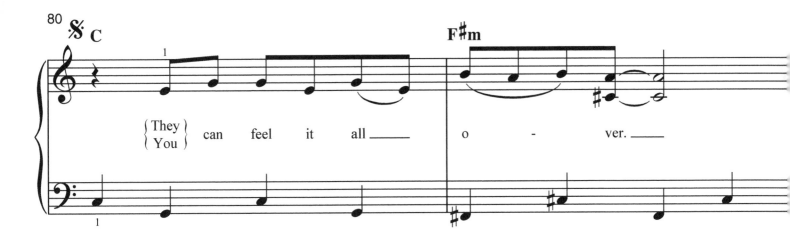

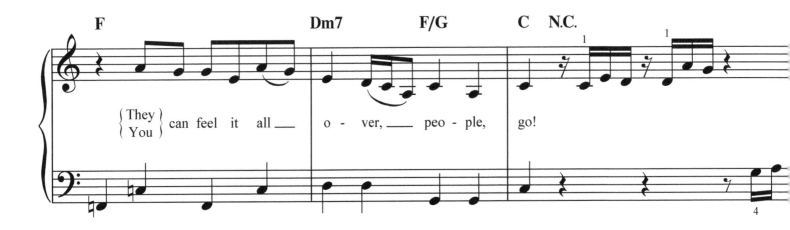

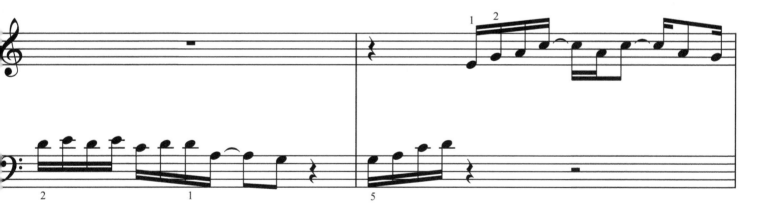

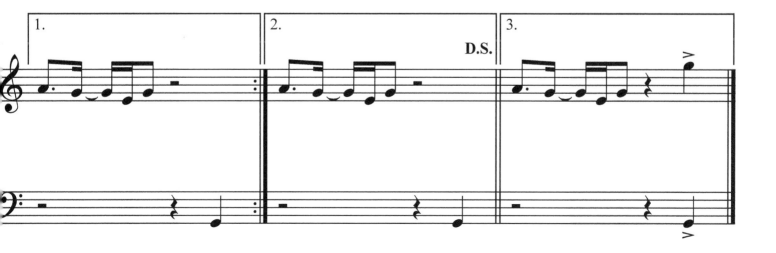

WE WILL ROCK YOU

Words and Music by
BRIAN MAY

Moderately

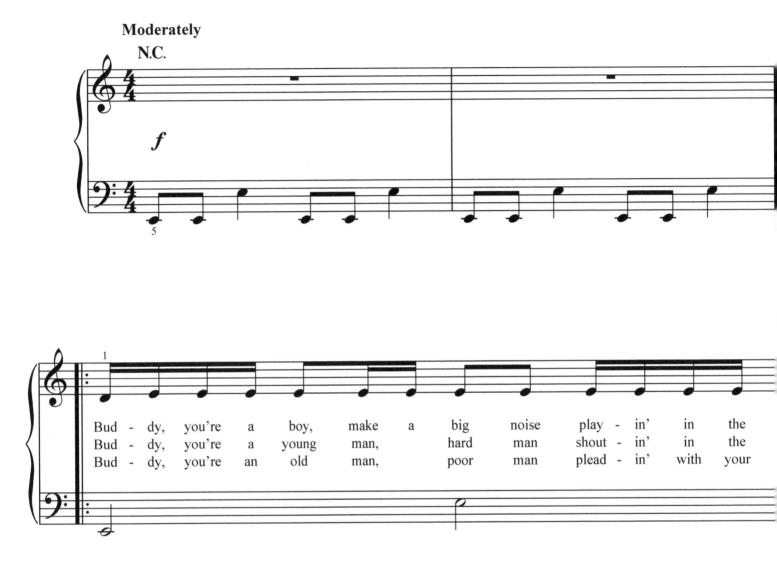

Bud - dy, you're a boy,	make a	big	noise	play - in'	in	the
Bud - dy, you're a young man,	hard	man	shout - in'	in	the
Bud - dy, you're an old man,	poor	man	plead - in'	with your

street.	Gon - na	be	a	big	man	some - day.	You	got
street.	Gon - na	take	on	the	world	some - day.	You	got
eyes.	Gon - na	make	you	some	peace	some - day.	You	got

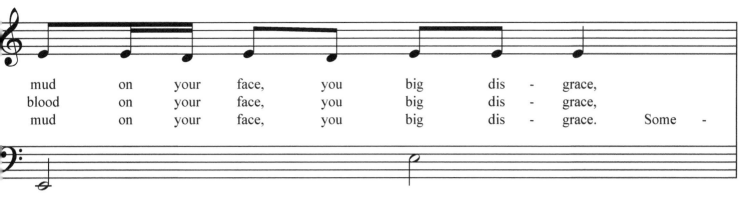

mud on your face, you big dis - grace,
blood on your face, you big dis - grace,
mud on your face, you big dis - grace. Some -

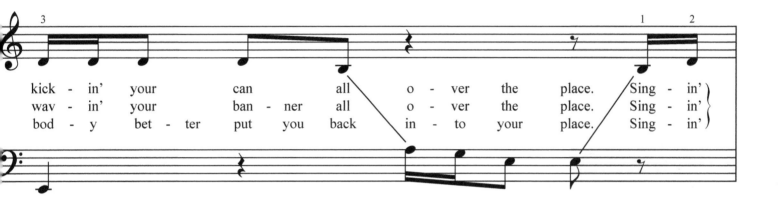

kick - in' your can all o - ver the place. Sing - in'
wav - in' your ban - ner all o - ver the place. Sing - in'
bod - y bet - ter put you back in - to your place. Sing - in'

1., 2.

we will, we will rock you. _____ We will, we will

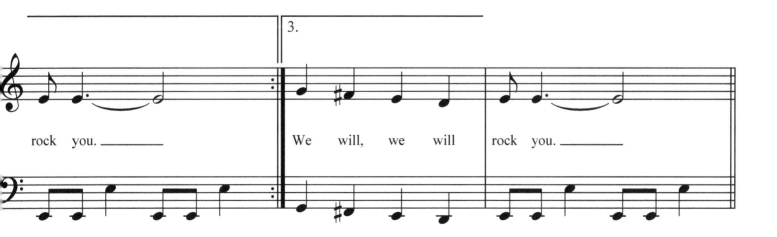

3.

rock you. _____ We will, we will rock you. _____

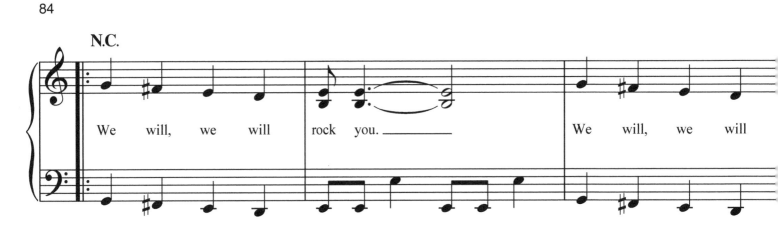

N.C.

We will, we will rock you. ___ We will, we will

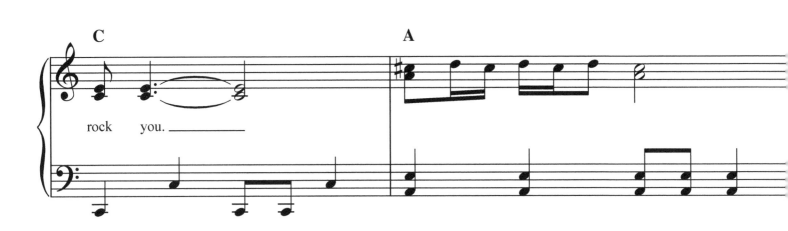

C   **A**

rock you. ___

1.   2.

WALKING ON SUNSHINE

Written by
KIMBERLEY REW

Bright Rock

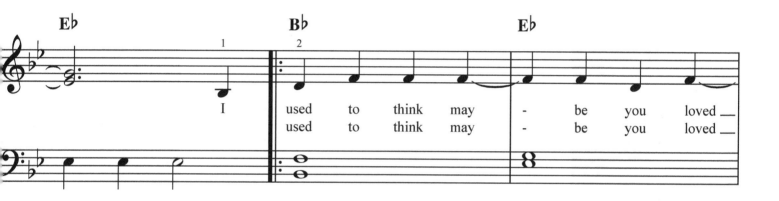

I
used to think may - be you loved ___
used to think may - be you loved ___

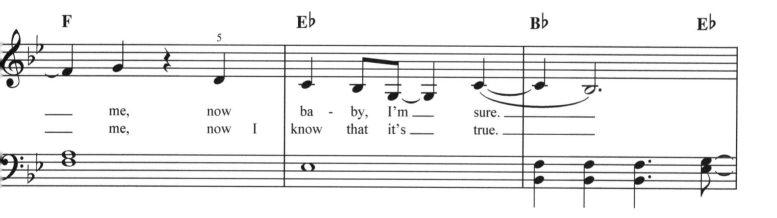

___ me, now baby, I'm ___ sure. ___
___ me, now I know that it's ___ true. ___

And
And I

I just can't wait _____ till the day _____ when you knock _____ on my door. _____
don't wan - na spend _____ my whole life _____ just a - wait - ing for you. _____

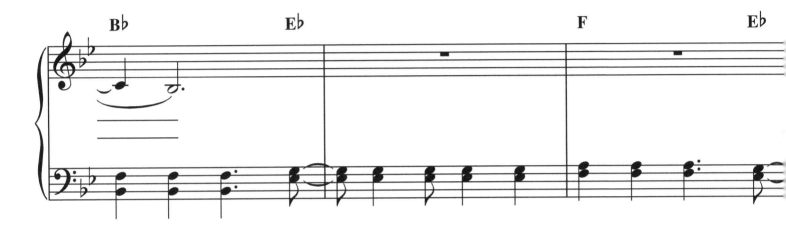

Now _____ ev - 'ry time I go for the mail -
Now I don't want you back _____ for the week -

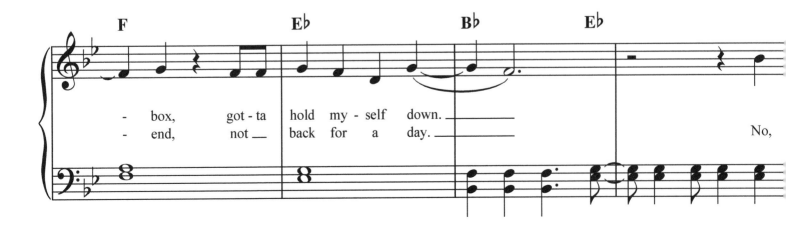

- box, got - ta hold my - self down.
- end, not _____ back for a day. _____

No,

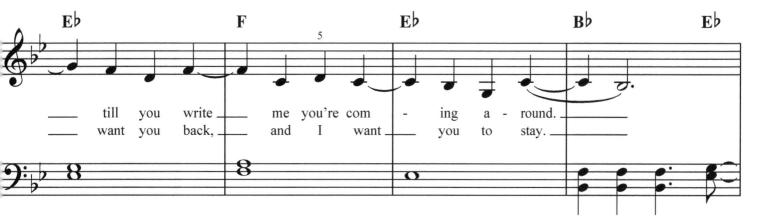

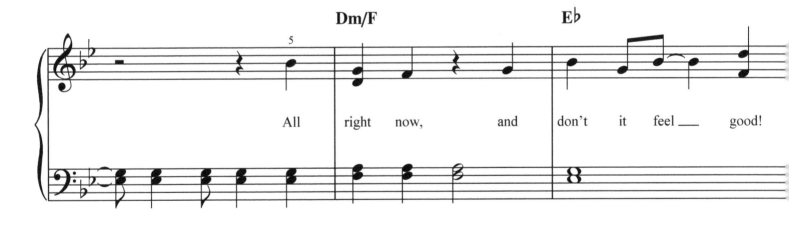

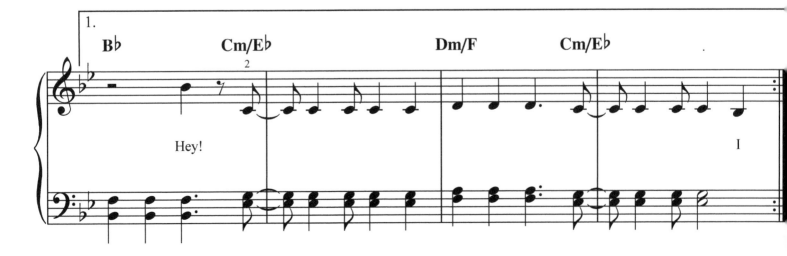

Yeah!   Oh,   yeah, ___ and   don't it feel ___ good!

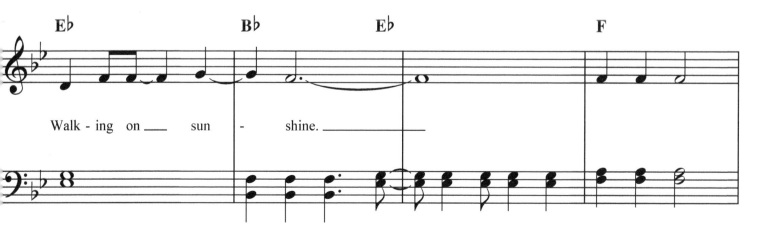

Walk - ing on ___ sun - shine. _____

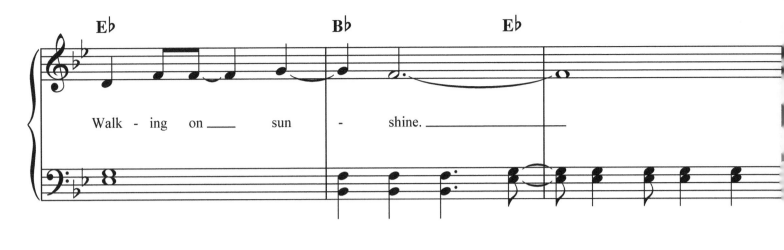

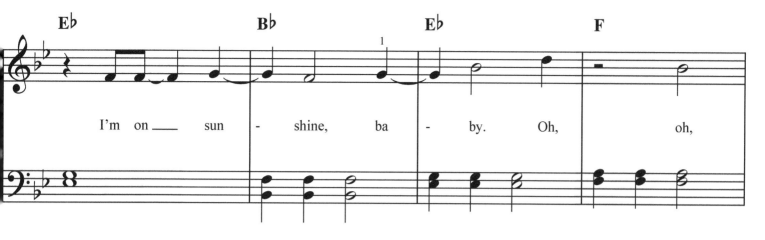

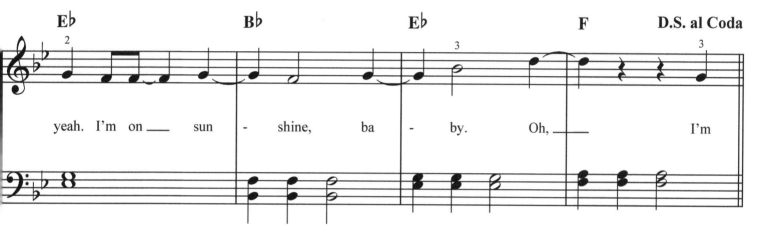

WE ARE THE CHAMPIONS

Words and Music by
FREDDIE MERCURY

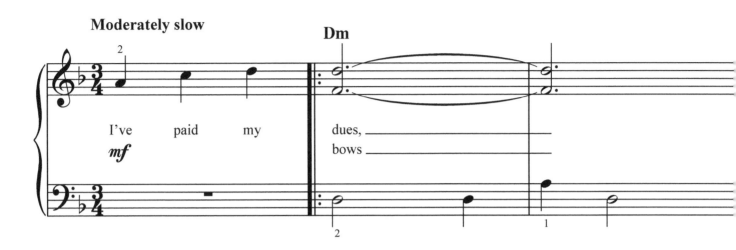

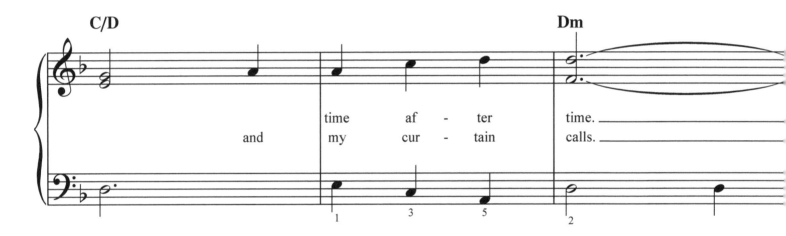

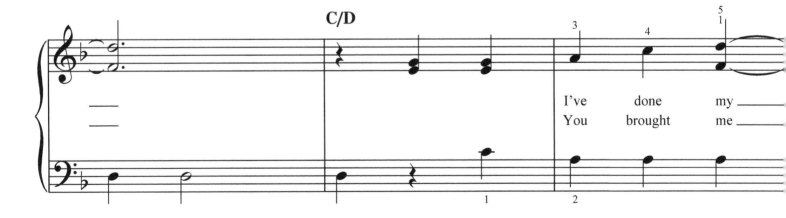

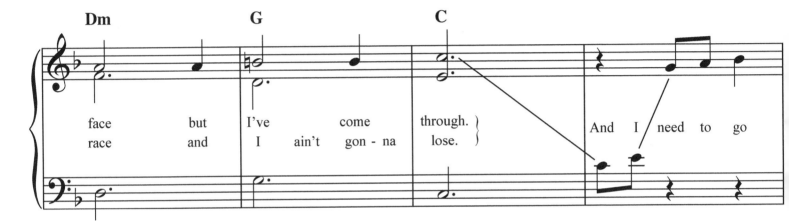

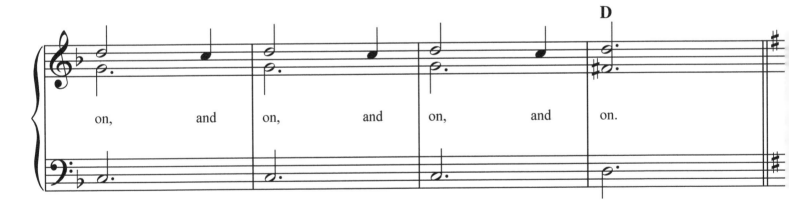

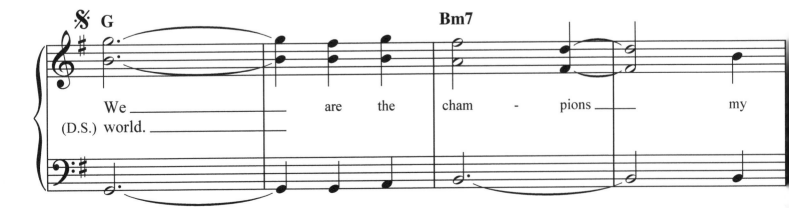

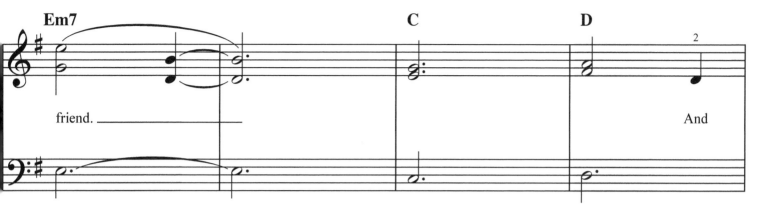

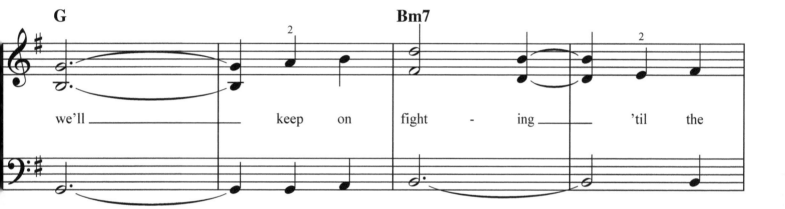

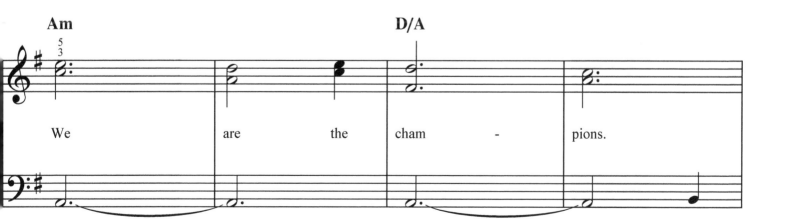

We are the cham - pions.

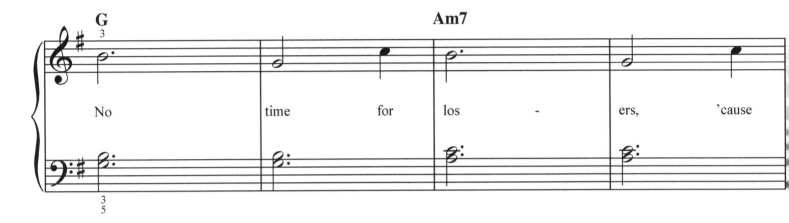

No time for los - ers, 'cause

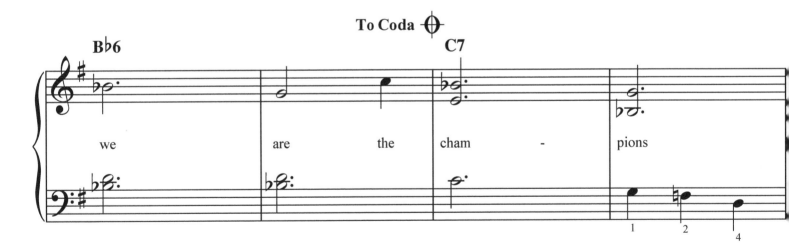

we are the cham - pions

of the world.

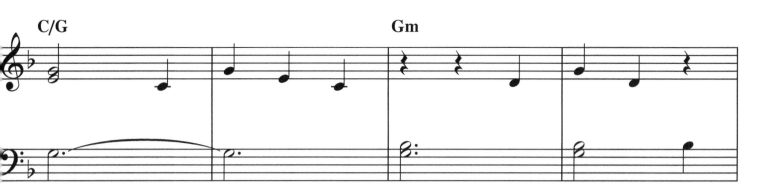

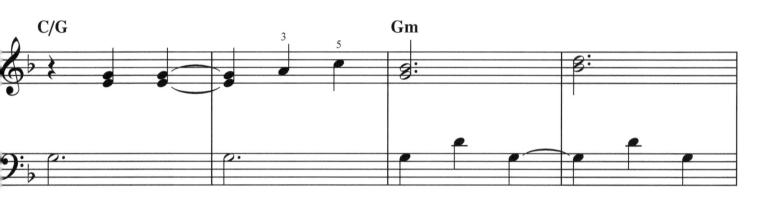

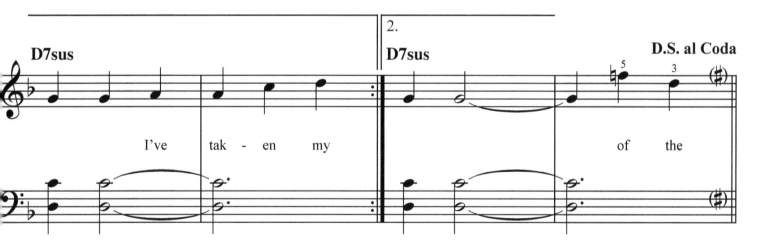

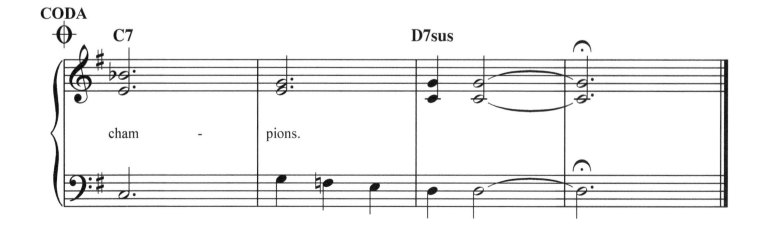

WE GOT THE BEAT

Words and Music by
CHARLOTTE CAFFEY

Moderately fast Rock

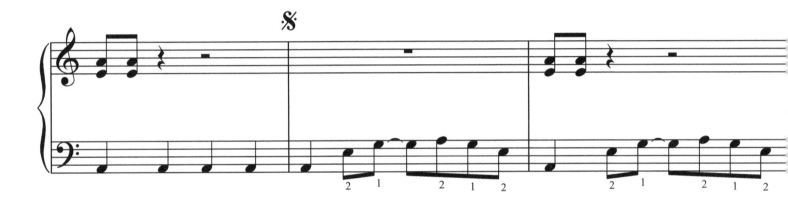

See the peo - ple
See the kids just
Go - go mu - sic

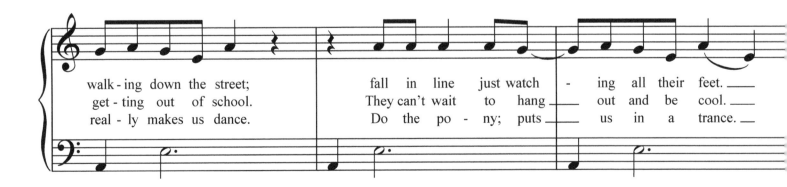

walk - ing down the street;   fall in line   just watch - ing all their feet. ___
get - ting out of school.   They can't wait to hang ___ out and be cool. ___
real - ly makes us dance.   Do the po - ny; puts ___ us in a trance. ___

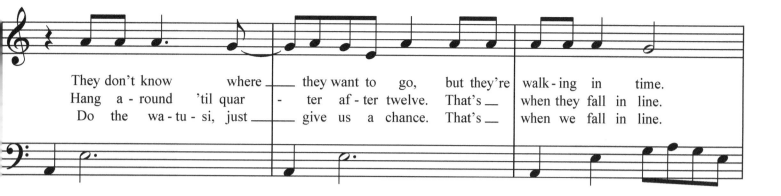

They don't know where _____ they want to go, but they're walk-ing in time.
Hang a - round 'til quar - ter af - ter twelve. That's ___ when they fall in line.
Do the wa - tu - si, just ____ give us a chance. That's ___ when we fall in line.

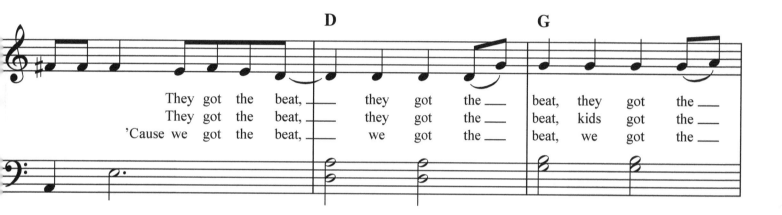

D   **G**

They got the beat, ___ they got the ___ beat, they got the ___
They got the beat, ___ they got the ___ beat, kids got the ___
'Cause we got the beat, ___ we got the ___ beat, we got the ___

F   **To Coda** ⊕ **C**   **A5**

beat,   yeah, they got the beat.
beat,   yeah, kids got the beat.
beat,

2

B

D.S. al Coda

CODA

C **A5**

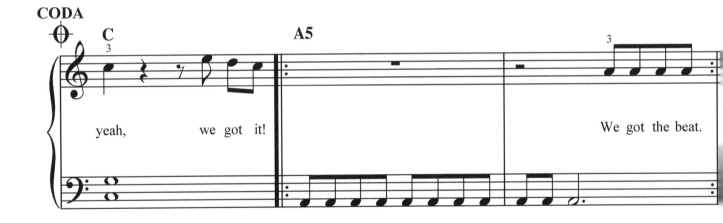

yeah,   we got it!   We got the beat.

Ev - 'ry - bod - y   get on your feet. (We got the beat.)   We know you   can

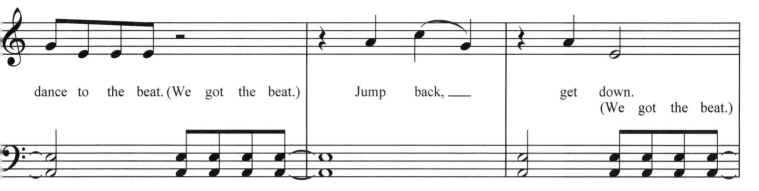

dance to the beat. (We got the beat.)   Jump back, ___   get down.
(We got the beat.)

E   **A5**

'Round and 'round and   'round.   (We got the beat.)   We got the beat.

(We got the beat.)   We got the beat.   (We got the beat.)

(We got the beat.) We got the beat.   (We got the beat.)   (We got the beat.) We got the beat.

WILD THING

Words and Music by
CHIP TAYLOR

Moderately slow, with a beat

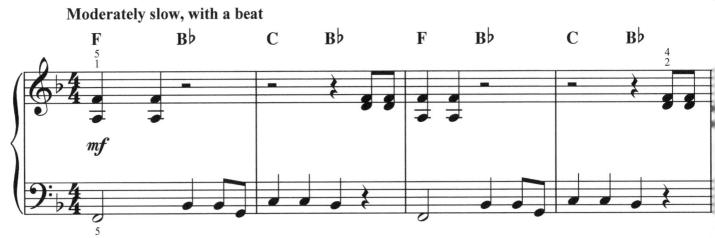

Wild thing,   you make my heart sing.   You make

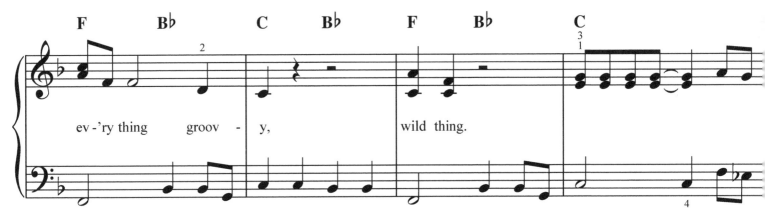

ev-'ry thing groov-y,   wild thing.

Wild thing, I ___ think I love you.
Wild thing, I ___ think you move me.   But I wan-na
    But I wan-na

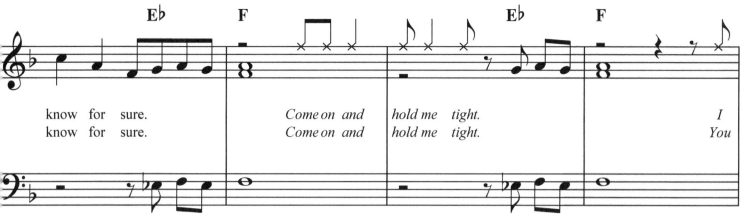

know for sure.
know for sure.

Come on and *hold me tight.*
Come on and *hold me tight.*

I
You

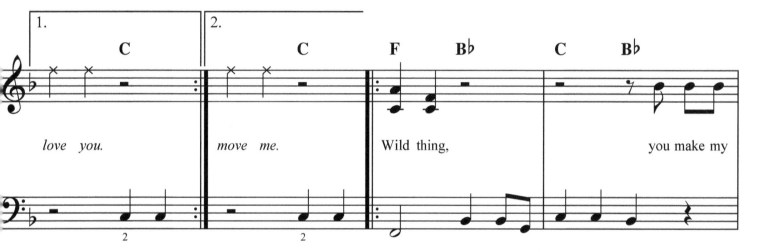

love you.

move me.

Wild thing,

you make my

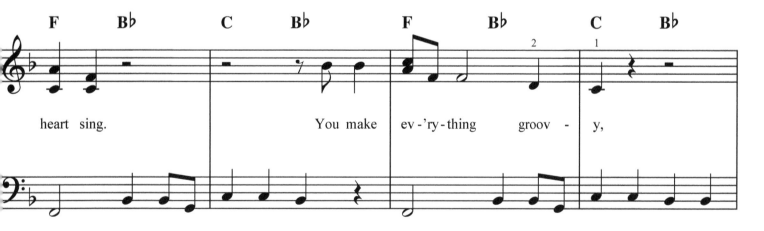

heart sing.

You make ev-'ry-thing groov - y,

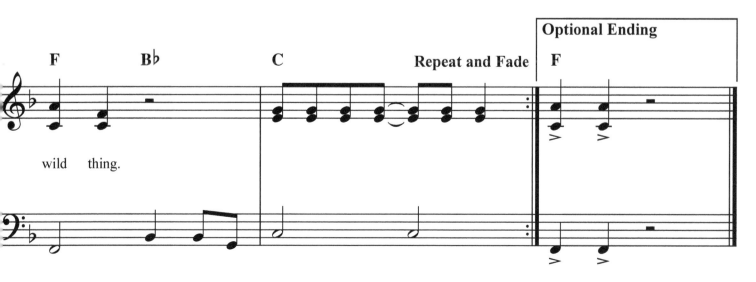

wild thing.

Repeat and Fade

Optional Ending

YOU'RE MY BEST FRIEND

Words and Music by
JOHN DEACON

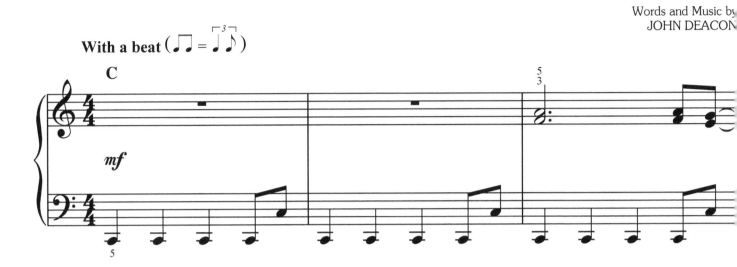

Ooh, you make me live ___ what-
Ooh, you make me live ___ when-

ev-er this world can give to me. ___ It's you, you're all I ___ see. ___
ev-er this world is cruel to me. ___ I got you to help me for-give. ___

Ooh, you make me live ___ now, hon-ey,
Ooh, you make me live ___ now, hon-ey,

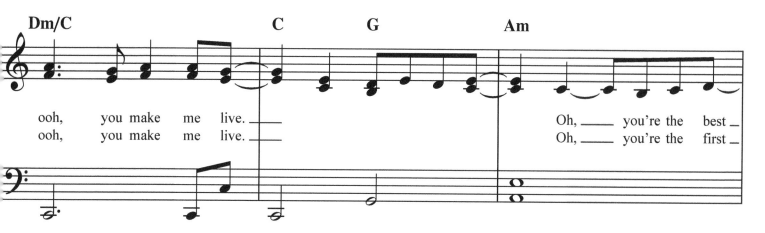

ooh,   you make   me   live. _____
ooh,   you make   me   live. _____

Oh, _____ you're the   best _
Oh, _____ you're the   first _

_____ friend   that I _____ ev - er had. _   I've been with you such a   long _
_____ one when things _____ turn out bad. _   You know I'll nev - er be lone -

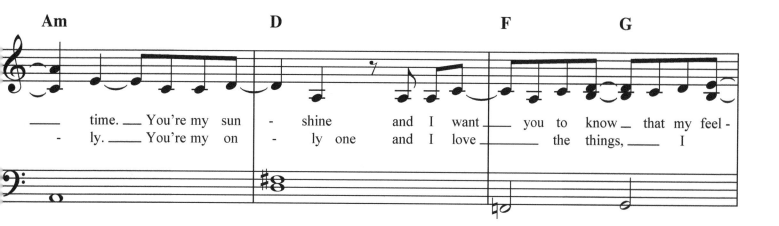

_____ time. _ You're my sun - shine   and I want _ you to know _ that my feel -
- ly. _____ You're my on - ly one   and I love _____ the things, _____ I

- ings are true: _____ I   real - ly love   you.
real - ly   love _ the   things _ that   you _ do.

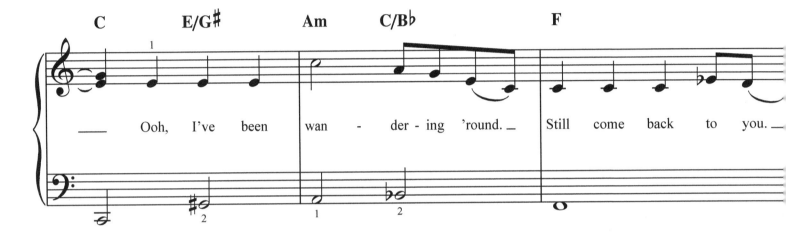

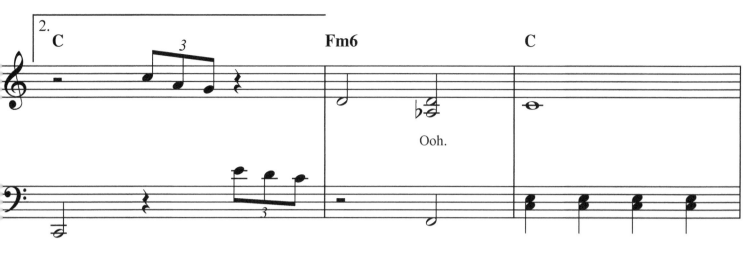

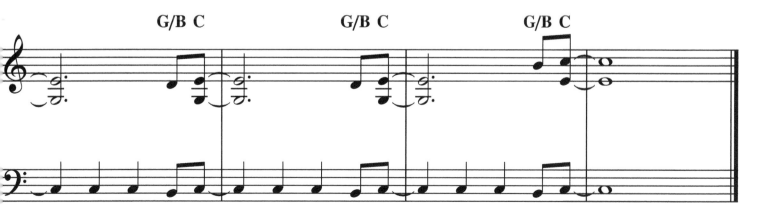

WHAT I LIKE ABOUT YOU

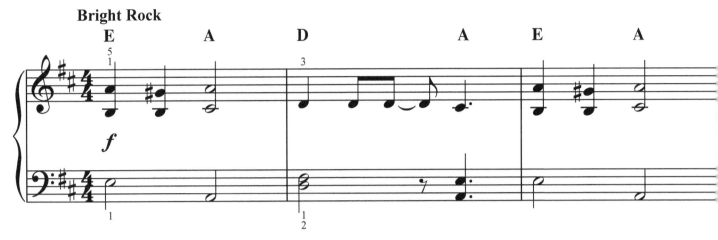

Words and Music by MICHAEL SKILL,
WALLY PALAMARCHUK and JAMES MARINOS

Bright Rock

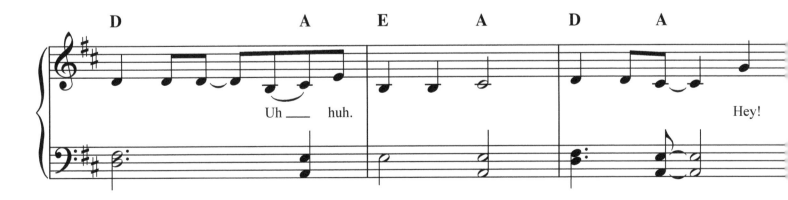

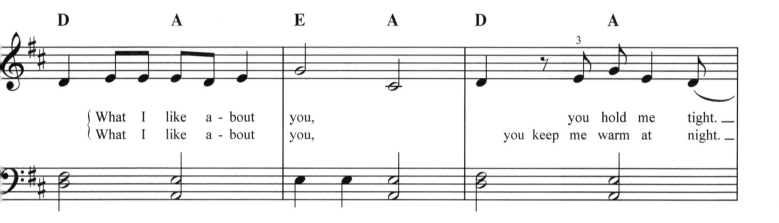

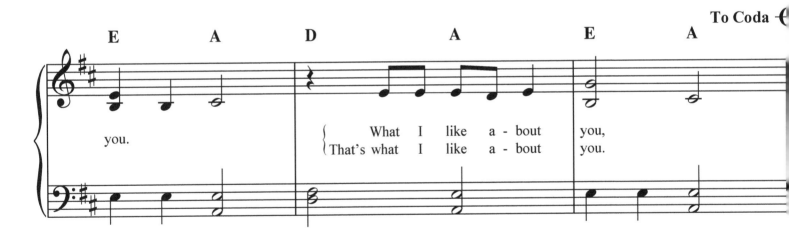

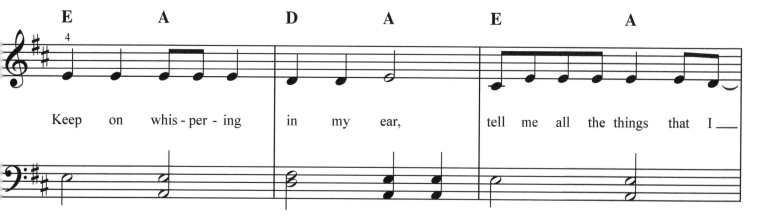

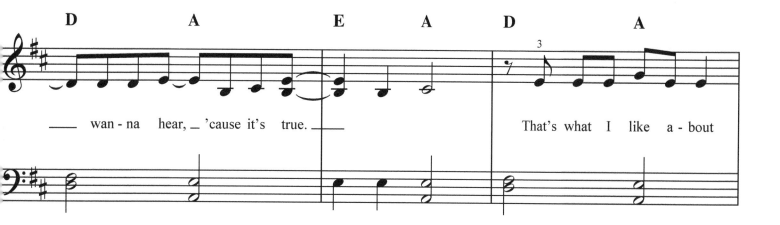

D.C. al Coda

CODA

That's what I like a-bout

you.

That's what I like a-bout you.

Hey!

Uh — huh.

Hey!